Minnesota Memories 2

by Joan Claire Graham

and

34 Friends

This is a collection of stories about real, not fictional people, places, impressions, and events. The writers lived in places like Albert Lea, St. Paul, Odin, International Falls, Adrian, Robbinsdale, Winona, Hastings, Lismore, Kenneth, Milaca, Owatonna, Northfield, Austin, Gilbert, Eureka, St. Clair, Henderson, Atwater, Minneapolis and Duluth. These are 48 extraordinary stories from 35 ordinary folks.

With tones ranging from hilarious to melancholy or merely reflective, 35 writers convey an impression of what it is to be grounded in the Midwestern culture of the 20th century.

Minnesotans will relate to stories about school events, summer pastimes, backyard theatrical productions, neighborly kindness, neighborly spats, unusual jobs, a moment in the spotlight, heroic acts, pets, town characters, hunting and fishing, small town life, family customs, colorful relatives and the incredible situations into which we are sometimes thrown.

Although many stories in this collection are about as funny as any you'll ever read, writers do not caricature or make fun of those experiences and customs we hold dear. There are no hotdish jokes or stories about Ole and Lena. These stories ring true because they honestly reflect our collective memory of life in the North Star State. And those reflections need no exaggeration or embellishment in order to be as good as they really are.

If you are from Minnesota, you will recognize kindred spirits and familiar settings. Don't put this book down. Curl up in an easy chair and have a good read. What the heck? Even if you grew up somewhere else--like Iowa--Wisconsin--or even the Dakotas-- we think you'll enjoy *Minnesota Memories 2*.

Thanks to the following for submitting their stories and photos:

Arlene Syverson Ayers
Marilyn Mikulewicz Baranski
Rebecca Braasch
Russell Christianson
David Chrz
Nicholas John Cords
Menno Dammer
Lloyd Deuel
Albert Eaton
Wayne Eddy
Madonna Erkenbrack
Myrle Solomon Erlich
Marion Field
Rich Geary
Gene Grazzini Jr.
Bonnie Broesder Hauser
Winnifred Kaercher

Joyce Kennedy
Wallace Kennedy
Bernice Lanik
Donald Matejcek
Kathy Megyeri
Robert Montrose
Maria Murad
Vicki Nelson
Suzanne Nielsen
Mabel Nordby
Arvin Rolfs
Lavonne Swanson
Steve Swanson
Tarrie Swenstad
Arthur Thompson
Virginia Anderson Trethewey
Donna Pierce Woodward

Cover photo taken at Lake Ely in 1948, by Aquinata "Cookie" Graham with her little box camera.   Thanks, Mom.
Back cover photo by Leah Nell Peterson, Cannon Falls Beacon

Thanks to the following people who helped.
Ron Margulis, RAM Communications, Joyce Kennedy, George Lanik, Cathy Wilary at Carlson Company Inc.
Cassandra Blizzard and Christie Phillips at National 4-H Council
Newspaper reporters and radio announcers who helped get the word out to storytellers all over Minnesota.

Minnesota Memories 2

ISBN: 0-9711971-1-3

Minnesota Memories 2

Table of Contents

Standing Ovation
by Joan Claire Graham

Long before Tyrone Guthrie built his famous theatre in Minneapolis, and a few years before the University of Minnesota Centennial Showboat raised its first curtain, and before the Stagecoach Players rode into Shakopee, the Water Street Theatre received a standing ovation from a capacity crowd in Mary Niebuhr's basement in Albert Lea.

The Albert Lea Festival and Civic Theatres are now located at Broadway and Water Street in downtown Albert Lea. The Water Street Theatre, founded years before the inception of either of those formidable groups, hit the boards only one night in the summer of 1953-- at the other end of Water Street, in the basement of Herb and Libby Niebuhr.

Company members consisted of neighborhood kids who had polished off two weeks of vacation bible school before settling into the serious business of getting through the dog days of summer. Parents, who feared we might contract polio at the beach, encouraged us to play quietly in our neighborhood, so we decided to put on a show. It had worked for Mickey Rooney and Judy Garland, so we figured it would work for us.

For a group of young kids, we had impressive resumes. We had all learned to read and write, as the youngest two of us had just finished first grade. Susan Voigt and I had recently made our live theatrical debuts in LeRand Studio's dance recital, "Stars of Tomorrow," and we interpreted that title as a prophecy. Not only were we stars of tomorrow, but we still fit into our costumes from yesterday. I had outgrown my tap shoes, but believed I could squeeze into them for one last dance. Most of us took piano lessons, Mary Niebuhr was well on her way to becoming the best young musician on the block, and all who had finished fourth grade played flutophones. Carol Adair and Pauline Hayes were aspiring actors, and just like Hollywood stars of today--everyone wanted to produce and direct.

Libby Niebuhr, who sang at weddings, funerals, and band concerts, appreciated the arts and tolerated our presence in her home during weeks of rehearsal. She served occasional refreshments, but like all parents in those days, refrained from meddling.

Niebuhrs' basement was the chosen venue because it was the least objectionable of all available basements. Nobody had a recreation room downstairs, so everybody's basement contained an old wringer washing machine with tubs, a large furnace with big ducts, clotheslines, exposed floor joists, spider webs, pipes, old National Geographics and cement floor. Though many theatre troupes would have considered those esthetic drawbacks prohibitive, we took them in stride.

Our basement was unsuitable because of its coal bin and stacks of old lumber, an outboard motor lashed to a post and a toilet sitting out in the middle of the room with no walls around it. Voigts' had a darkroom that couldn't be disturbed. Adairs' basement was comprised of many small rooms, and Pauline's basement was wet. All basements were cool in the summer and provided havens from swarms of hungry mosquitoes so, all things considered, Niebuhrs' basement was not that bad.

Like many aspiring summer stock companies, our first task was to prepare the venue. Brooms and mops took care of dust and spider webs, and willing volunteers cleared old magazines and discarded toys from the largest room. Mrs. Niebuhr hung her wash outside during summer months, so she didn't need her indoor clothesline. All company members donated the use of their family's picnic blanket for the grand curtain. Held in place with wooden peg clothespins, five ragtag blankets filled the sagging clothesline. A few safety pins here and there more or less closed off holes we made earlier in the summer when we used those blankets for outdoor tents and poked clothespin stakes into their edges. What it lacked in color continuity our curtain more than made up for in shabbiness.

Producing and performing our show kept us busy for weeks-- writing, rehearsing, publicizing and setting up the theatre. We used crayons and old cardboard to make programs, posters, and tickets and traveled the neighborhood knocking on doors and inviting neighbors.

Occasionally we got into a big fight over artistic differences and ended up not speaking for a day or two. But eventually, through hard work and determination, the big night arrived and the stars of tomorrow played to a packed house.

Audience members who entered Niebuhrs' back door and carefully descended steep basement stairs, chose a seat from among an assortment of kitchen and folding chairs, benches, and striped canvas camp stools arranged in two rows. They noticed the colorful curtain, pointed, and shared information about who owned which picnic blanket pinned to the clothesline. I think this activity established fellowship and put them in a good mood from the get-go.

We charged admission and sold popcorn and Kool Aid, and we were shocked by the size of the turnout. At least twenty friends, neighbors, and relatives crowded into the theatre that evening. Folks from as near as the Niebuhr household and as far as the Klostermans from RR 1 showed up. Grandparents and babies attended. Publicity was successful and the buzz must have been irresistible.

As someone dimmed the lights by pulling a chain on the overhead bare bulb in front of the curtain, an attentive lighting technician shined a flashlight on the Master of Ceremonies, who welcomed audience members and introduced the first act. The audience was immediately amused and charmed by our cleverness. This was going to be a great evening of theatre.

Pauline, Carol, Susan, and Mary performed the opening skit about a dysfunctional family. I don't know where any of us got the inspiration for that one. The gist of the skit was that Mother and Father, intent on reading their paper and eating breakfast, were perturbed by their bratty children and didn't know what to do with them. Father, while in the act of dealing out corporal punishment, got his comeuppance when his suspenders slipped off and his pants fell down--much to his chagrin and the delight of his children. Then, to their added delight, Mother's knickers fell off right there in the kitchen as the whole scene dissolved amid chaos. I don't even want to think about the Freudian interpretation of this dramatization. The actors hammed it up as audience members laughed and clapped. Energized, we entertainers moved on to a musical interlude.

I sang "Chicago, Chicago, that Toddling Town" and tap danced-- a capella--dressed in a green tap costume decorated with itchy silver glitter. Mary played her flute, and Susan danced the hula. I put on another costume and sang "Trees" based on the poem by Joyce Kilmer, and when I looked at Ethel Jones, who lived across the street, she was weeping in the front row. I didn't find out until years later that her tears were caused by trying to suppress laughter she thought would surely hurt our feelings. Carol recited all the poems she could remember, and Pauline told some knock-knock jokes, We all sang a few songs together, did the Hokey-Pokey, and prepared for the grand finale--a fashion show.

There had been a fashion show at the mother-daughter banquet, so we all figured we knew how to do fashion shows, and it was our collective artistic impression that fashion shows topped off the evening the way people wanted evenings to be topped off.   Never mind the fact that we had no sense of fashion, nor did we even own any clothes that weren't hand-me-downs that everybody hadn't seen a hundred times,

We had dragged anything that remotely resembled a costume into the basement that night, and in the short time the show had been in progress, we had all made a couple of costume changes behind the picnic blanket curtain. The fashion show gave us one last excuse to change outfits.

Someone put a scratchy record on the portable phonograph that sat backstage on the laundry table, and the models approached the run-way. The first models met friendly applause from audience members as they walked to the center and turned for approval to the stylish strains of Guy Lombardo and his Royal Canadians. Nothing says "cutting edge fashion" like the melodic strains of "The Tennessee Waltz."

My cousin Kathryn Klosterman was about 2 years old, and we all thought she was adorable. Even though she had not attended rehearsals, we wanted her to participate in our fashion show, so we had instructed her mother to bring her to the show all dolled up.   The choreography for the fashion show went like this: Each model came from behind the curtain on stage left, crossed to stage center, turned once to show off her outfit, and exited stage right.

We all knew little Kathryn would not be able to learn this intricate choreography, so I devised a plan that I thought would trick her into at least crossing the stage in her cute little outfit. Somebody deposited the tiny child at stage left and called her attention to a lollipop I held temptingly beneath the curtain from behind. This attracted her interest as I thought it would, but my plan backfired.

As Kathryn reached for the lollipop, I surreptitiously crawled along behind the curtain keeping the candy just out of her reach. Crawling on Niebuhrs' basement floor like this was tricky because I was wearing a dress with a hoop skirt for the fashion show.

Kathryn really wanted that lollipop, so she kept reaching and squatting, standing up, stooping, reaching, whining, reaching again, and finally stomping and screaming. I hadn't counted on the frustration factor and certainly hadn't counted on anybody screaming during our grand finale. I simply thought the candy would entice her across the stage, and I thought nobody in the audience would notice the bait. They definitely noticed, but fortunately Kathryn's screams were drowned out as the Water Street Theatre audience exploded with laughter and applause.

As the audience reaction reached its apex, I peeked out through a safety pinned hole and noticed Ethel Jones weeping again. Her nose glowed red and her hanky was soaked as she wiped her eyes, and she finally put her hands over her face and her head in her lap.

At the conclusion of the fashion show, when all the models lined up onstage, audience members rose to their feet and cheered while cast members bowed, curtsied and smiled from ear to ear.   Kathryn clung tenaciously with both hands to her yellow loop-stick lollipop as we passed around a Skippy peanut butter jar for donations to the Sister Kenny Foundation. One generous benefactor not only donated to the charity but additionally gave each cast member a nickel for a Popsicle.

The Fountain Street Grocery Store was still open that evening, and we knew that both root beer and lime flavored Popsicles had arrived in stock recently, so we strolled down there and bought Popsicles which we divided in two so we could share both flavors.

We walked around the block wearing our costumes, eating Popsicles and rehashing the highlights of our performance. I took off my tap shoes to ease my blistered toes and walked barefoot in the early evening.

We talked about Mickey Ahern, a surprise attendee who had spitefully dumped his popcorn all over the floor because, he said, it gave him asthma. We talked about the lollipop disaster. We wondered how much money we had collected in the peanut butter jar. When the subject of Mrs. Jones came up, Mary Niebuhr said seriously, "I think Mrs. Jones was crying because she doesn't have any children," and I believed Mary's interpretation for many years.

The next day we struck the set, tidied Niebuhrs' basement, and took our picnic blankets home. Rave reviews poured in from across fences and over telephone lines.

"Great show!"

"Be sure to let us know the next time you perform."

"You guys have so much talent."

And we believed those encouraging words and felt a great sense of accomplishment. As we grew older, we all became involved in high school band, theatre, talent shows, chorus and music recitals. Some of us went on to perform in college groups and civic theatre. I wrote and directed plays, and all of us developed an appreciation for the performing arts.

A couple of days after the show, we phoned the director of the local Sister Kenny Foundation chapter and arranged to hand over the proceeds of the Water Street Theatre's Summer Extravaganza. Mr. Obert Chalstrom wore a suit and we dressed up and met him in the lobby of the Albert Lea Tribune building on South Broadway.

A Tribune photographer posed us and snapped a picture as we gave Mr. Charlstrom our peanut butter jar containing $3.64 to help fight polio. The Tribune, however, didn't print that picture until November. Tribune editors probably had a lot of other newsworthy charitable bequests or show biz benefit stories to cover that summer, but the important thing is that our local media eventually ran the story and noted our largesse.

A Tribune photographer posed us and snapped a picture as we gave Mr. Charlstrom our peanut butter jar containing $3.64 to help fight polio,

That donation must have come in handy for the folks at Sister Kenny's Foundation. Just a few years later, Jonas Salk developed his polio vaccine, thus eliminating for us kids the threat of that dreaded disease. Going to the beach became safer, except for the fact that none of us could swim.   So until we rounded the corner from childhood to adolescence, most of us continued to spend our summer time playing in our neighborhood.

The Water Street Players attempted to produce other shows, but always got bogged down with scheduling difficulties, casting squabbles, budget problems and artistic differences. No Water Street Theatre encore was ever staged in Niebuhrs' basement, which was probably all for the best. No show could ever top our inaugural season that summer of '53, so it was good that we retired in the glow of critical acclaim.

Hit the Slopes; I Wanna Be Hip
by Joan Claire Graham

As the 60's wore on, a record number of single baby boomers exploded onto the professional scene. As men faced military service, women began to view careers as something to do rather than something to come back to after raising kids. Nearly all college grads in the mid 60's got hired by a school district or company because recruiters visited our campuses, scheduled interviews, and offered us contracts months before we even graduated. Although signing a contract was easy, the prospect of actually growing up was daunting.

Having signed those contracts and agreed to teach school or work for the Man, we became members of the very establishment we had only months before protested and mistrusted. Therefore, we needed to preserve our youthful identity by seeking social activities far away from our older co-workers

We were hip and they weren't, so we needed to nurture that hipness in our social lives. Without spouses, kids or house payments, we had some discretionary income to spend for recreation and entertainment. Though I had been a victim of hip bypass throughout my high school and college years, I joined the ranks of young professionals in the 60's, so I thought it might not be too late to become hip.

Hip baby boomer professionals went to bars with live bands on weekends to meet and dance with other hip baby boomers. I could do that. Hip baby boomers moved into new apartment complexes with exercise rooms and swimming pools, and they joined health clubs where they met other hip baby boomers. They bought stereo components, attended movies at downtown Minneapolis theatres, grew long hair, wore bell bottoms, mini skirts and long crocheted vests. The guys grew sideburns, bought new cars, and hosted weekend parties where they served drinks made in blenders. Up to that point, I was on the hip track, just waiting to break into the ranks.

But suddenly hip baby boomers took a turn for which I was unprepared. They began to hit the slopes. They spent endless hours talking about skis, ski wax, tow ropes, chair lifts, boots, poles and bindings. They bought expensive skis and togs, spent weekends at Lutsen or Sugar Hill, and came back to work Monday with lift tickets still stapled to their jacket zippers.

At this point, I began to lose sight of becoming hip. Since I had never skied, I felt recreationally challenged and unhip. We had no hills in Albert Lea where I grew up! Unless I wanted to be left behind socially, I had to catch up and learn at age twenty-three. Every hip Minnesota baby boomer professional had to know how to ski.

Not wanting to make a fool of myself among friends, I scoured the Minneapolis Tribune for news about lessons for beginners. I planned to take a few lessons and join my friends for a ski weekend after making all my stupid mistakes in the company of strangers. Although I doubted that I would ever become an expert, I felt that with a few lessons I could at least join the hip crowd on the slopes and afterwards at the chalet.

I found what I needed--a package deal at Hyland Hills in Bloomington for lessons and equipment rental on three consecutive Monday nights in January. The timing was perfect, since a hip young teacher named Bryce was organizing a bus for a ski trip to coincide with Lincoln's Birthday.

My lessons required a long drive on a school night, but my chance of running into anyone I knew was slim, and Hyland claimed to be the perfect place for beginners. Since the advantages outweighed the drawbacks, I signed up for three lessons and looked forward to merging into the hip crowd during the long weekend in February.

Purchasing my outfit was the best part of the whole experience, since I am a savvy and enthusiastic shopper. I looked good that Monday evening as I bid my roommate good-bye and set out in my '67 Falcon for lesson #1. Even by Minnesota standards, the weather that evening was brutal, with a temperature well below zero, and the car failed to warm up as I drove. It was not until I was halfway there that I realized my car would not warm up because its thermostat was broken.

By the time I arrived at Hyland Hills, I could no longer feel my feet or hands. Undaunted, I sprang from my car and hobbled towards the chalet, where a friendly team of young professionals measured me for boots and skis. Since I was running a little late, they saved time by strapping me in before I knew what was going on. My lower extremities were still numb, so I didn't even realize I was geared up until they pointed to the door and told me to join the class of new skiers standing by the teacher with a red cap. I suspect they had a good laugh watching my skis tangle and my arms flail as I tried to extricate myself from the chalet.

Once outside, I was confused and disoriented. From speakers wired to poles and trees, popular music from a local radio station blared so I couldn't hear what people were saying. Although the dark slope was illuminated by a few spotlights, it was difficult to see who, if anyone, was wearing a red cap. For one thing, I'm slightly night blind. For another, in this subzero climate, every time someone spoke, he or she was drowned out by music and immediately enveloped in a vapor cloud. And finally, everything out of the direct ray of the spotlight looked either black or white. Several groups stood around, and after shouting questions to strangers, I finally found a row of novice classmates standing in a long row in front of a guy who looked like he wore a black cap surrounded by a cloud.

As I took my place in a line of a dozen skiers, I felt glad that my lesson was only an hour long because the severe cold was turning what might have been joy into sheer torture. My frozen feet started to throb with pain as exercise thawed them slightly, and my nose and cheeks stung in the frigid air. As my frozen fingers tried to grip ski poles, my eyes watered, my nose ran, and my nostrils froze together whenever I tried to sniff. Reaching into my pocket with frozen fingers and a ski pole fastened to my hand to retrieve a Kleenex proved impossible. I resolved to tough it out no matter what, because I wanted to learn to ski so that I could be hip. Over the strains of Jimi Hendrix, the instructor said something I couldn't understand, and, as if in a dream, my eleven classmates magically began to float forward.

"How are they doing that," I asked myself incredulously, "without even moving their feet?" Just then an evergreen tree swallowed me from behind. My back hitting the trunk jarred my senses, but I couldn't believe my predicament.

From between snow-laden boughs I could just barely see all the other skiers some distance away, still standing in their straight line apparently listening to the instructor. What I had perceived as their forward movement had been an illusion. They hadn't been gliding forward; I had been sliding backward--backward into an evergreen tree. Apparently my disappearance went unnoticed, since nobody even glanced back in my direction. Worse yet, with music and noise made by people having fun, nobody heard my cries for help in that god-forsaken frozen tundra.

From my sylvan trap, I caught sight of my group again. This time they were moving their feet and skiing forward--putting more distance between where I was and where I was supposed to be. There I was, stuck at the base of a tree on a ski slope on what must have been the coldest night of the century--half frozen and without a clue how to free myself. Luckily, I was wearing a nice new fashionable outfit.

I yelled for help, but my cries were futile. I tried shaking branches to attract attention, but the shaking released from the boughs a shower of loose snow that covered my already frozen head and body. Next I tried moving my feet forward, but the ground sloped upward from the base of the tree trunk, and I did not know I should move my skis sideways up the slippery incline, so my attempted forward progress was like walking on a treadmill--energy expended without progress. Embarrassment turned to frustration and fear. Pine needles scratched my face, frigid air froze my hands and feet, darkness enveloped me, and nothing I tried worked.

After struggling for what seemed like an eternity, I decided that if I wanted to avoid freezing to death in a tree at Hyland Hills, I would have to try something desperately unhip. My skis and boots were still on my feet, my poles were still strapped to my wrists, and since I had not participated in putting them on, or even watched the process, I had no idea how to ditch this equipment. My fingers were frozen stiff and I started to cry, which made my plight more pathetic and my frozen face colder. This was definitely not hip.

In desperation, I sat on my butt with my legs bent and skis out to one side and, shielding my stinging tear-streaked face from an attack of killer pine needles, I inched myself sideways up the little rise and out from under that tree. I struggled up from the ground and made it fifty yards to the chalet, where nobody noticed my dazed and disheveled appearance.

After I sat on my frozen hands for a few minutes, they loosened up enough so that I could figure out how to remove the boots and skis. Without a word, I turned in my equipment to a teenage guy who was having such an important conversation with a cute girl that he forgot to ask why I was leaving before the end of my lesson.

I crawled back into my frozen Falcon, remained frozen during the ride, arrived home around 9 p.m., told my roommate not to ask why I looked so much worse than I did when I left the apartment in my cute new outfit, and thawed myself out in a hot bath, where I reflected that my road to hipness had definitely taken a detour. As I began to feel life in my extremities, the humiliation of the night's events gave way to optimism and good humor. There remained two more ski lessons in my series of three. Improvement seemed inevitable.

Temperatures soared into the twenties during that next week, and I replaced my car's thermostat. More snow fell during the weekend, and I felt hopeful about lesson #2. In fact, I felt so confident that I put down a deposit for Bryce's February group ski getaway. When I awoke Monday morning, however, I disappointedly learned that the mercury had fallen below zero again, but I figured that tonight's lesson held more promise if I at least arrived at Hyland Hills unfrozen. The worst part about ski lessons was undoubtedly behind me. This week I would learn how to ski and become hip.

I arrived early and took time to ask the chalet folks to show me how to fasten my own boots and bindings, and I introduced myself to the instructor, a young hip guy named Jeff, who might possibly be charmed by my gender and helplessness. Immediately I felt more in control--less anonymous. At least Jeff knew my name and might think to look for me if I disappeared.

Jeff said he had not seen me at lesson #1. I had suspected this, but I was relieved to learn that he had not left me in that pine tree for spite. He showed me how to walk uphill sideways--an important lesson I had missed when I was attacked by the tree last Monday--and asked if I had any questions. I didn't even know what to ask, and I didn't want to seem like a dolt, so I decided to lag behind and watch others who attended the first lesson and copy whatever they did.

Across tonight's Arctic air, I strained to hear Jeff's words, which were nearly inaudible because of the music and noise from 10-year-olds schussing and playing with skill and abandon. Tonight's lesson, I just barely heard, would include snow plowing down a hill after using a tow rope to go up it. I thought Jeff was making some kind of lame joke about plowing snow, but believed I could learn to hang on to a moving rope without pulling my arms out of their sockets. In my spiffy outfit I started to believe I could get the hang of all this and eventually become hip.

I leaned back and ascended a small hill with ease, but was surprised by how much bigger that little hill looked from the top. I heard Jeff say, "Remember to snow plow," but, having missed the first lesson, I had no idea what he was talking about and thought it was some kind of inside joke because skiers pray for snow, and snow plows take snow away.

A half dozen of my classmates, their skis pointed into a V shape, awkwardly made their way down the hill. To me they looked silly and tentative, not like the skiers I'd seen on ABC's Wide World of Sports.

"Wow, I thought, I know I can do better than that!" With skis pointing directly downhill, I pushed off and began my descent. Before I knew what was happening, my speed accelerated and I experienced the sickening sensation of being entirely out of control. Directly in front of me was a row of people waiting for a tow. Beyond them stretched a chain link fence. It would be good if I could stop before smashing into either, but I didn't know how to stop or even slow down.

"Snow plow!" yelled Jeff. What the heck was he talking about?

At full speed I plowed into the tow line, knocking people like bowling pins this way and that. Minnesota nice turned sour as epithets and screams flew through the crisp night air and elbows and knees landed on the packed snow. My victims, who were not amused, attacked my intelligence, my attitude, and my ancestral lineage.

Luckily, nobody was injured, but I was too embarrassed to try again, so I trudged off to the chalet, checked in my equipment, and drove home. I began to reassess my desire to become hip and wonder if I had the nerve to show up for lesson #3. On Friday I decided I wouldn't, but by Sunday I thought I might.

But I didn't have to make the decision. The gods intervened and sent an ice storm Monday that closed schools early and cancelled lessons at Hyland Hills. When a Hyland employee called and asked if I'd like to reschedule, I declined. Not only that, but I threw in the towel on the quest to become hip. Bryce returned my deposit for the February trip, and my snazzy ski outfit gathered dust in the closet. I probably missed out on a lot of good times because I never joined my friends on the slopes. On the positive side, my friends were probably safer and better off without me.

Baby boomers eventually married and had kids of their own, producing another baby boom. I merged into the mainstream of my generation at that point, when it didn't matter to anybody that I had been unhip in my younger days. I joined a generation of Minnesota professional women who feverishly worked to become supermoms who could do it all--careers, carpools, kids, homes. And at that point in my life I could do it all--all except ski.

The Front Porch in Albert Lea
by Joan Claire Graham

Hot, sultry summer Minnesota days dragged on miserably endless in the 50's. Our twelve-inch oscillating electric fan tried to move stagnant humid air and provide relief, but it had far more work than it could handle. If mother cooked anything--and she always did--the heat in the house surpassed miserable and became unbearable.

The only air conditioned places in town were the Broadway and Rivoli theatres, whose penguin-adorned signs seduced movie goers with the tease, "It's Cool Inside." Icicles dripped temptingly from the o's in the word "cool," as if Minnesotans in July, so long removed from winter, needed a visual reminder of what "cool" meant. Since our family could not live in a movie theatre, we moved out to our front porch.

Old houses had porches and new ones had breezeways, and everybody used them. Other generations and cultures said, "patio," "veranda," or "lanai," but we said, "porch."

When friends asked for directions to our house in Albert Lea, I told them put their backs to the fire station and go west past Central Park, down the hill past the high school, over the tracks and into our front porch. Water Street ended at our porch that stretched across the front of our house on First Avenue.

A canopy of elm boughs provided shelter from the morning sun, keeping our porch shaded and comfortable all day. Elms on both sides of Water Street formed a perfect arch that not only framed and shaded the neighborhood but camouflaged our spying eyes from those we observed. In addition to affording respite from summer heat, our porch provided an excellent vantage point for watching the comings and goings of traffic on two streets.

My sweaty dad rocked in his red metal chair after working all day at the packing house. He snickered and mocked neighbor men who wore shorts and sandals, and he thought it was okay to sit bare-chested and criticize them--as long as he wore long pants.

As he observed the neighborhood, he'd make comments and ask questions to no one in particular:

" How many times has that Loken girl gone out with that guy this week? How old is she?"

"Is Mrs. Brown going to have another baby? How old are their other three kids? "

"How many miles to the gallon do you suppose Sorensons get with those old Cadillacs?"

"If those Minehart kids keep playing out there in the street, one of them is going to get run over."

Occasionally we'd hear band music and see Cap Emmons leading his high school marching band down Water Street in their summer drills. The sound and sight prompted kids to run outside and join the parade. Little children marched on the sidewalk playing imaginary drums or twirling stick batons. Sometimes, when the wind blew west, we heard music wafting from open windows as the band played in their high school band room above the auditorium. We'd look down Water Street expecting to see marchers, and remark that the wind must be blowing just right.

A guy we called Limpy walked by several times daily, always wearing the same brown pants, brown hat and beige shirt. He walked all over town all day every day and earned his nickname because of his strange gait. Some said he limped, and others said he obsessively pulled his pants leg away from his shoe every three steps. We never asked his name and didn't know where he lived, but he was a part of daily life, and he nodded hello and tipped his hat. We frequently speculated on some aspect of his outfit, his walking regimen, his state of mind, or his gait.

The elderly Johnsons quietly swayed on a wide swing on their porch next door to the north. The Voigt family porch on the other side had regular windows that closed during winter. Niebuhrs at the end of Water Street had a glass-window porch with a fold-down couch for summer sleepovers. The Sorenson and Jones family porches were located at the backs of their houses. Our porch was designed with a three-foot ledge about twelve inches deep that enclosed the lower half on three sides and provided a place to park our junk--much to my tidy mother's disliking. Screens extended from the top of the ledge to the ceiling.

The front porch was the most comfortable and social room in our house--for a few weeks each year. During cold months it gathered dust and snow, but during late spring and summer, our porch was paradise. The casual vinyl and aluminum furniture wore no starched doilies, the throw rugs could be machine washed, the painted wooden floor was durable, and restrictive house rules against noise, food, and roughhousing didn't apply.

My dad screwed two metal o-rings into the wooden tongue-and-groove ceiling. With an S hook, Mom attached a chain connected to a wooden swing seat ordered from Montgomery Wards' catalog. The porch swing didn't wobble like outdoor swing sets, so I fearlessly pumped it high enough to touch my toes to the ceiling. Whenever necessary, if we needed more floor space, I unhooked the chains and put the swing away.

We ate supper on the front porch nearly all summer. I'd set up the card table mom got with Green Stamps, arrange chairs, and mix a pitcher of Kool Aid--our preferred summer beverage. We'd haul food and dishes out to the porch, set pitchers and platters on the ledge, eat supper around 5 o'clock, and finish washing dishes by 6.

As evening temperatures dropped a few degrees, kids played tag, statues, kick the can, starlight moonlight, or kick ball outside until dark or until mosquitoes became ravenous enough to attack us through layers of repellent Mom always bought from the Fuller Brush man.

As darkness approached, we'd either walk over to Hayek Park to watch the Albert Lea Packers play baseball or attach an extension cord to the radio and listen to the game on the porch. If there was no game, we'd walk down to the band shell by the lake to hear a concert, beg Dad to drive us to the A & W or Dairy Queen for a cool treat, visit the porch of our cousins across town, entertain company on our porch, or simply spend the evening on our porch listening to radio music or exchanging greetings with neighbors in other porches.

We seldom used the overhead light because we didn't want to attract insects. The street light in front of our house provided as much light as we needed, and from among the tree branches we watched with terrified fascination as bats swooped this way and that in search of their nightly feast.

Across the street, members of the Rol Sissell band sometimes filled the night with dance music as they rehearsed in Sorensons' living room. Bill Sorenson practiced his trumpet upstairs--songs like "Stormy Weather" sounded romantic in the summer air.

Two or three evenings each summer, we welcomed the mosquito sprayer truck as it drove by spraying a stream of DDT up to the trees and down to the ground. Nobody warned us to go inside and shut the door, and although the odor of the spray was slightly unpleasant, we did not realize its toxic effect on ourselves or the environment. We only saw the short term effect--freedom from mosquito bites for a few days.

In addition to providing relief from summer heat, our porch was a window to the world. What did we see from that window? We saw our neighbors coming and going in their accustomed patterns. Families, dressed in their finest, piled into cars on their way to Sunday church. A little boy on Water Street drove a little red peddle car instead of a trike.

A steady stream of music students came and left from Helen Sorenson's house, clutching their red John Thompson piano books. Boys and girls, dressed for the prom and looking like magazine models, emerged from their own porches one Friday each spring to stand briefly outside with their dates, while moms snapped photos that still exist in someone's album. Denny Adair, who had Down Syndrome, rode his bike around the block every day, waving to people he knew.

One day a car hit Midge, and I watched a teenage boy dash from his house on Water Street, tearfully scoop up the mortally wounded little black dog, and implore her not to die. Neighbors who passed back and forth to three nearby corner grocery stores advertised the availability of Popsicle flavors and often triggered a copycat purchase.   Red Randall and another guy played catch with baseballs in the street and stepped aside whenever a car approached.

From the intersection of two roads, we affirmed when life was normal and served as eyewitness when it was not. Neighbors came and went, raising their window shades in the morning and pulling them at night. Men mowed lawns and raked leaves. Kids rode bikes, played hop scotch and roller skated. They fell down, picked themselves up, and returned with bandaged knees. Babies learned to walk, and old folks started using canes.

Evening thunderstorms drove us back into the house, but on clear nights we'd set up cots and lower the back of the old chaise lounge--haul pillows and blankets from the unbearably hot upstairs bedrooms and sleep on the front porch. Dad never slept there, but my brother, my mom, my sister and I slept there night after night. The three-foot ledge masked sleepers from passers-by, and the little hook and eye lock on the screen door made us feel safe.

There was a wonderful time before sleep when I'd listen with heightened awareness to night sounds--the slam of a car door, approaching footsteps on the sidewalk, the faraway wail of a siren, bark of a dog, or rumble of a train on the tracks one block away. Then, feeling secure, I'd drift off to sleep. When I awakened, just before dawn, the air would be miraculously cool enough to necessitate pulling the blanket up to my chin. The milkman stopped his truck, and bottles clinked as he put two quarts in our silver milk box on the front steps. Birds sang reveille to another hot day, and my mother insisted that we get up and restore the porch to its daytime mode before we shamed her by presenting a disheveled first impression to anyone who might come to our door.

Crickets' evening song signaled the beginning of the end of summer in August. In a few weeks we'd move indoors, sleep in regular beds, eat at a regular table, use the porch merely as a transition between outside and inside, and resume our rigid school year regimen. Neighbors would be able to come and go under less surveillance, and television would provide a different kind of window to the world.

In the late 60's, an Albert Lea Tribune photographer recorded the removal of our stately elm, Freeborn County's first Dutch Elm Disease fatality. Our neighborhood vista widened when trimmers cut down that first tree, and in the following summers, almost all the trees on First Avenue and Water Street died.

Without leafy boughs to camouflage their flaws, those old houses looked naked, shabby and embarrassed. Without the shadows that masked our curious interest in everybody's daily business, we felt self- consciously exposed-- lined up in chairs watching our now-stark neighborhood from the porch-- spotlighted by the sun in the morning and the street lamp at night.

As the late 60's ushered in a new social consciousness, we retired from our porch, and our porch retired from the house. Dad paid Sears to install   steel siding on the house and converted the front porch into a regular room. He tore out the ledge, took down the swing, carpeted the floor, draped the windows, installed electrical outlets, a heater and an air conditioner. Upholstered chairs, a sofa bed and an assortment of lamps replaced old aluminum furniture, and the former porch became a room for all seasons--less interesting but more modern, more practical, and definitely more socially isolating than the old front porch.

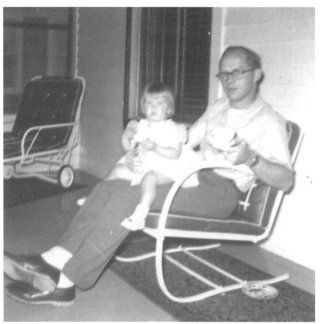

The front porch was the most comfortable and social room in our house--for a few weeks each year. The casual vinyl and aluminum furniture wore no starched doilies, the throw rugs could be machine washed, the painted wooden floor was durable, and restrictive house rules against noise, food and roughhousing didn't apply.

Great Expectations, 1956
by Joan Claire Graham

When I was 10, I had no idea how babies were conceived, but I loved babies and I wanted one. I thought God sent babies to lucky people who said the right prayers, so I prayed that He would perform a miracle and send me or my mom one as soon as possible. I dreamed of this miracle.

I tirelessly played with tiny cousins, treated my dolls as if they were real, and imagined how it would be to have a real baby. The baby Jesus in my mother's Christmas creche actually looked like a newborn, swaddled and helpless, and each December I made him tiny blankets that I tucked around to keep him warm.

One afternoon late in the spring of 1956, my mother confided a startling fact. She said that she was going to have a baby. She took me in as a confidante and told me this important news in a solemn discussion as we lay on her bed. She had been tired and worried for months, and in a state of depression and concern, she told me about the baby. I was certainly not mature enough to understand her state of mind, but over the years I've had plenty of time think about what she went through.

The family doctor Mom consulted when she thought she might be pregnant removed a polyp and said she was experiencing the first sign of menopause. But as months went by, pregnancy became obvious. As a 45- year-old teacher of retarded children, Mom was aware that older mothers often had unsuccessful pregnancies or gave birth to abnormal children. She interpreted the doctor's initial inability to detect her pregnancy as a sign that either she or the baby was going to die. She did not want to share her frightening premonition with friends or even family.

I heard "baby" and hoped for the best, but my ecstasy contrasted with Mom's agony. It was all I could do to keep from jumping on the bed screaming my joy to the heavens. My prayers had been answered. God was sending a miracle! Mom stifled my jubilation by telling me God would send a curse if I didn't stop counting unhatched chickens. She would tell her brother and sister. She let me tell my dad, my brother and my grandmother, but I had to take a vow of secrecy and not tell one other

soul. This was just what I needed in a childhood already repressed beyond belief by rules and religion. But in accordance with her wishes and
fearing God's wrath, I told nobody else this incredible secret.

When fourth grade ended after Memorial Day, I went off to
Mankato to spend time with Grandma Sally, who was supposed to teach
me to sew and bake bread. Mom thought she might not survive this pregnancy, so she wanted me to bond with my grandmother and learn some
life skills.

But my grandmother was not a patient woman, a teacher, or a
pessimist. Instead of teaching, she just made me some doll clothes and
baked clover leaf rolls. I fell under her optimistic spell, and we discussed
names as we sat around eating those delicious rolls with homemade jam
and listening to Perry Como sing "Hot diggity dog ziggity boom what
you do to me," on the radio. Sal liked Phoebe, while I thought it would
be neat to name the baby Polly, in honor of the Polyp.

By the time I returned from Mankato, Mom's pregnancy was in
full swing, but her mood had darkened. She wore regular clothes until
June, but had to sew a few summer maternity smocks. Now that she
looked pregnant, her fear intensified and she went underground.

In a town the size of Albert Lea, it was difficult for a person as
well known as she was to avoid being seen. She made my dad drive her to
a church in Austin. While there, she confided to a priest she didn't know
that she felt a sense of impending doom and was too afraid and ashamed
to deal with sympathy and scrutiny from people she knew. Recognizing a
woman in a fragile emotional state, the priest gave her a dispensation from
attending mass.

With that obligatory weekly public appearance out of the way, Mom
had to devise excuses to avoid other social contacts. Some neighbors knew,
but they didn't travel in her circles or attend the same church so she thought
they wouldn't pose a security threat. Her social contacts were reduced
by the fact that he didn't teach or meet with her bridge club during summer months. She didn't drive so she sent me off on my bike to buy anything she needed--supplies that included everything from fabric to Bit
O'Honey bars to Camel cigarettes whose smoke clouded her gloomy days.

I almost spilled the beans a few times because this huge secret could be revealed in so many contexts. Once, when I saw a maternity smock pattern exactly like the one my mother had, I remarked, "Oh my mom has..." Then, realizing I was about to reveal classified information, I groped for an end to my sentence... "an old violin in the attic." It was better for me to appear to be completely nuts than to tell this secret.

Mom sat around the house most of the summer, feeling increasingly morose, detached and frightened. We were not allowed to paint a nursery, buy baby clothes, discuss names or make any plans. As August wore on, Mom told me that her due date was the first week of September--the beginning of the new school year.

Though she didn't want to discuss her condition, she finally had to tell directors of the Freeborn County Association for Retarded Children that her medical situation would prevent her from resuming teaching early in September. They agreed to postpone school, and she agreed to come back to work as soon as she could. Her premonition of doom cast serious doubt that there would be a baby to care for--even if she survived delivery.

A couple of days after I started fifth grade, my grandma rode the Jefferson bus to Albert Lea, and my dad and I picked her up at the Hotel Albert. She took the bull by the horns and jump started the nesting activities that Mom was too paralyzed to carry out. She told Mom to buy some supplies and get ready for a baby. Although I dared not hope, for fear of tempting a vengeful God, my grandmother's attitude suggested that my mom's fears might be unfounded.

The next morning, Dad took Mom to the hospital, but when I came home from school she was sitting on the front porch--with no baby. My fear flared, my hopes dimmed, but they flickered back to life later when she wrote a list of baby supplies and told me to go to Penneys and buy those items only after the arrival of the baby. What an important responsibility for a child not yet 11 years old!

On a beautiful Saturday morning, September 8, I awoke early and noticed my mom was gone again. I tried to stifle my hopes and fears, though my heart was pounding. My brother was still sleeping out on the front porch, my grandma was visiting relatives across town, and my dad, who was going about his routine business, told me that he had dropped Mom off at Naeve Hospital around 6 a.m. Dropped her off--like a car for points and plugs--when she felt like she was taking her final walk!

Around 9 o'clock, with my anxiety level soaring, I convinced my dad to phone the hospital. He took his time before dialing the number. As I watched his face for clues, the person who answered told Dad that Mom was doing well after giving birth to a 7 pound 13 ounce healthy baby girl around 8 a.m. Much to my dad's dismay, I received the news by jumping around the house screaming with unbridled joy and relief before bolting out the door to tell everyone I could find. What a choice bit of gossip that must have been for those who hadn't seen Mom all summer and didn't even know she was expecting! On my way out of the house, I stopped to tell my sleeping 15-year-old brother, who disappointed me by grunting and telling me to shut up and let him sleep.

Children were not allowed to visit hospital patients, so I had to keep myself busy and wait nearly a week to see my little sister. As soon as stores opened, I walked down to Penney's with Mom's list and bought three little flannel nightgowns with snap fronts and ribbed cuffs. I bought six little undershirts, three dozen diapers, some plastic pants, two receiving blankets, a bonnet and booties. The clerk laughed at the belly bands on my list and told me to tell my mom that belly bands were no longer considered necessary.

When word of my sister's birth got out, friends and relatives responded with a generous outpouring of gifts that made September seem like Christmas. Members of the Rosary Society, families of retarded children Mom had taught over the years, former classmates, relatives and friends sent darling little nylon dresses lined with pastel slips, hand knit sweaters, two-piece terry pajamas called Nappies, little shoes, sheets for the crib, blankets, toys and money. Mom's bridge club threw a shower and gave her a high chair I later used for both my kids. Having a baby in the house turned out to be even more fun than I had imagined.

My dad allowed me to stay home from school the following Thursday when my mom brought my sister Ann Marie home from the hospital. In those days hospital personnel sent each baby home in a corrugated cardboard box with little lamb designs on the sides--pink for girls. People used to think I was kidding when I told them we brought the baby home in a box, but it was true.

The box was about two feet long with eight inch high sides. We fashioned a mattress from a folded blanket, set the box on the piano bench, and used it for a bassinet until we got proper nursery furniture.

On September 8, 1956, the anxiety that preceded the birth of my mother's last baby gave way to joy and relief. The baby was alive and well, and so was my mother. What a gigantic relief! All my imagined fun with a baby sister became reality. First I became a walking billboard for my baby sister by wearing pink clothes to school for three days. As time passed, I happily learned how to fold and change diapers, feed a baby, bathe a baby, rock a baby, burp a baby, talk to a baby. I took her for walks, showed her off, told her stories, and read her books.

When she got a little older, I taught her to sing popular songs, and I told her who sang all the tunes. Friends amused other friends trying to stump the baby with pop music trivia, but they never could. As soon as a new song came out, I taught her the name of the singer or group, and she always remembered. The corner grocery store owners gave us free candy when Pop Culture Wonder Baby entertained customers with songs and trivia. I had a blast with Ann. She was my first love and my last doll. She was worth all the anguish we had undergone throughout the summer.

I don't think it was uncommon for Catholic women who practiced the only officially approved method of birth control to have "change of life" babies when their body rhythms started to skip a few beats. Unlike many career women today who delay having children until their forties, the women of my mom's time thought it was best to have babies while they were in their twenties. Thirty-five was pushing it. Forty-five was dangerous and embarrassing.

My dad took a lot of ribbing. He got angry when the guys at the plant teased him about being a Romeo. Since he was nearly 50, you would think they would have hailed him as the man of the year. Today they probably would. My mother took a few knocks too. When a teenage girl at church remarked, "Your little granddaughter looks a lot like Joan," Mother was too embarrassed to explain that Ann was her daughter.

A few other forty-ish women we knew had babies after that; some had problems, and some didn't. A few months after my sister was born, one of Mom's friends had a Down Syndrome baby who died young. One bridge club member's baby died shortly after birth, but another member enjoyed her change of life baby so much that she had another healthy baby the following year.

I doubt that those other families went through their period of expectation under the cloud of apprehension that permeated our home throughout the summer of '56 . What's sad about my mom's depression and fear is that she had no social, medical, or psychological support to help her bear or overcome her feelings. She bit the bullet, bore the suffering, and spread fear throughout the family. What should have been a time of joy was a time of impending doom.

Prenatal care and diagnostic procedures have come a long way since then. Today's specialists could offer medical and psychological help to someone in my mother's frame of mind. But back then we got through the ordeal as best we could, feared the unknown, and heaved huge sighs of relief and thanked God when we heard the words, "Both mother and baby are doing fine."

I had a blast with Ann. She was my first love and my last doll. She was worth all the anguish we had undergone throughout the summer.

Tough Row to Hoe
by Joan Claire Graham

The Grapes of Wrath by John Steinbeck was a staple of the high school sophomore English classes I taught. As the Joad family left Oklahoma, hit Route 66, and scrambled for work as itinerant field hands, I drew a parallel to their miserable situation by telling my students about the time I worked as a field hand in Minnesota. I don't know if it taught them anything about the plight of downtrodden people, but my story kept my students quiet and attentive for a while. Holding the attention of today's kids isn't always easy, but this story did the trick.

In 1963, part-time jobs for teens were scarce in Albert Lea. Department stores and restaurants hired mostly full-time career clerks and waitresses, and the A & W and Dairy Queen hired only a few seasonal workers. Fast food joints hadn't been invented yet. Babysitting wasn't what it is now because most mothers stayed home with young children. Teenage babysitters earned twenty-five to thirty cents an hour--mostly on Friday or Saturday nights when they would rather be out spending money. On a good night, a babysitter might earn a dollar and a half.

By the time we hit high school, most of us wanted and needed part-time summer jobs. Not only did we have to buy new Bobbie Brooks coordinates for the upcoming school year, but we had to save for college and learn financial responsibility by managing our own money.

While we complained about our lack of summer employment opportunities, Mexican workers in Texas talked to recruiters and signed agreements to work as field hands on farms near Albert Lea. These workers, many of whom were women and children, traveled a thousand miles to Minnesota, where farm owners put them up in huts or cabins. They worked the fields from May through September and then returned to Texas. We hardly noticed these people in town because they lived in the country, and their children seldom enrolled in our schools. And if they did, they didn't stay long enough to make friends. They were almost invisible.

I suppose most of us town debutantes either disliked or ignored those dark-skinned girls who came to town Saturday nights with their boyfriends to watch the same movies we wanted to see at the Broadway. We stood in line to buy tickets with them, but we thought their lipstick was too red and their hair was too long. After the ticket taker let us all in, we took no further notice of their presence. They were temporarily among us, but we didn't know them and they didn't know us.

So it was without guilty conscience or any sense of social impropriety that we sat up and listened when word got around that one of the local sugar beet farmers had decided not to hire Mexican migrant workers. Apparently he had not been satisfied with them the previous year, so he decided to show the Mexicans that they were expendable.

His strategy was to hire town kids who needed summer jobs. Believe me, there were a lot of us. I had just finished my high school junior year and Sue Dania, a Greek exchange student who lived with us, had graduated and was marking time until the American Field Service rounded up all the exchange kids and headed them back towards their home countries. School was out and days were long. We wanted jobs.

The terms of employment at the sugar beet farm were fairly simple. We were to drive out to Hollandale, and the farmer would show and tell us everything we needed to know. Payment was cash, upon completion of work. Most of us had not even tended a garden prior to being hired as field hands, but we were excited and enthusiastic about learning. What this job lacked in glamor it made up for in fresh air and sunshine.

Friends picked up the two of us early on an overcast June morning. Sue had no more farming experience than I had. She was the daughter of an Athens tailor, and I was the daughter of a government meat inspector. We bought most of our fruits and vegetables at Boyd and Jacks.

We hopped into a car already loaded with four girls our first morning and drove out to the farm. Someone had suggested that in order to get good tans, we should wear swimsuits under our shorts and shirts. Nobody owned halter tops or tank tops like kids wear now, so the swimsuit was the garment of choice for catching rays. Sun screen hadn't been invented, and doctors were years away from telling us about the connection between sun exposure and skin cancer. We who wanted to maximize the sun's effect on our skin applied baby oil or olive oil.

Skies were cloudy that first day, but we hoped for a reprieve from rain. After all, we wanted to earn money and we wanted tans. The farmer who hired us was a big guy with a Dutch accent. He explained that today's work consisted of blocking sugar beet plants, which had started poking their way out of the soil and were now a couple of inches tall. Blocking beets, thinning them with a hoe-width between plants, consists of two motions. In the first motion, the blocker chops the hoe into the soil in front of the weeds and unwanted seedlings. In the second motion, she pulls those weeds and seedlings and soil forward so that unwanted greens are uprooted and destroyed. Blocking allows the surviving plants enough space to grow.

The farmer's little blonde daughter, about 8 years old, took delight in prancing up and down the rows, celebrating the fact that she didn't have to work and we did. She also pointed out inferior work to her father. She annoyed everyone from the start.

Pay was 45 cents a row. Rows were about a fifth of a mile long. The farmer said that he would only give us 30 cents for our first row because we were beginners doing inferior work.

Blocking wasn't easy for a beginner, and the constant bending and chopping caused back, arm, neck and shoulder pain. The soil was somewhat dry, which made blocking more difficult. We all started to chop and pull, chop and pull. I couldn't believe how many chops and pulls there were to a row. I'd look forward and back to see how much progress I had made, and it seemed like a lot of work got me nowhere. It took more than an hour to block a row.

Although he furnished hoes, the farmer did not furnish work gloves or even suggest that we might need them. When we asked for water, he grudgingly hauled out a common bucket, but admonished us to be sure to bring our own the next day. A couple of hours after we started working, storm clouds moved in, and we had to abandon our work and head for the car because there was no other shelter from the rain.

We sat in the car as lightning flashed, thunder crashed and rain lashed. Although the farmer probably wouldn't have minded if we had risked our lives and continued working, we finally decided to give it up and try again the next day.

As the next morning dawned with a beautiful golden late spring sunshine, we returned to the farm, eager to earn summer money and get great tans. Although we had sore hands, arms, necks and shoulders, we had gotten enough sleep and were ready to shake off yesterday and start fresh. We brought lunches and big thermos bottles filled with tap water, but we were otherwise ill-prepared for a full day's work. The shortness of the previous day had tricked us into feeling competent and confident that we could make a go of this summer job.

Mexican workers drove by early that morning, honking horns and yelling. The farmer expressed concern at their behavior, and we thought he had a point. We probably felt superior to those protesters and had no idea why they were making such a fuss.

We who had never experienced a full day of field work were about to learn a lesson that would last a lifetime. None of us had never gotten blisters from working, so we didn't bring gloves, bandages or antiseptic.

As blisters formed on our hands and feet, we learned that our employer had no sympathy or first aid supplies. The outhouse had no soap or hot water. Healing or administering to our wounds became the responsibility of our immune systems. We were too stupid to bring sun hats, and in search of the perfect tan, we bared our backs and basted them with olive oil. The sun beat down relentlessly, the hours wore on endlessly, and no storm rescued us. We were in for a long, hard day.

At first we were heartened by the simple fact that rain had loosened the soil and made blocking somewhat easier. As the day wore on, however, we city girls experienced what many workers in the world take for granted--back breaking, blistering, physical labor and the humiliation that comes from being exploited by a boss who knows he's the guy in charge of the only job you can get.

The good humor and girlish chatter we had enjoyed on our ride to the farm soon gave way to the sound of blocking beets--chop-rip, chop-rip. The farmer's little girl continued to run around pointing out errors, and we began to suffer aches and pains in places we didn't know had nerves. Every time we went up a row and down the next, we reported our progress to the farmer, who kept a tab. And although we were all working as hard as we could, he always made a negative comment about our slowness or ineptitude.

With an hour to go before our scheduled lunch break, and with most parts of my body aching with blister or fatigue, and five hours of servile labor behind me, I reached into my shorts pocket and found a lollipop--probably left over from a picnic I'd attended with my 6- year-old sister. What a find! With shaking hands I pulled off the cellophane wrapper and stuck the candy into my mouth. The sugary fruit flavor tasted delicious, but the little girl--probably jealous that I hadn't given it to her--considered my snack a snitchable offense and pointed me out to her father. He clomped over in his heavy boots and stood before me

"Kinda old to be eatin' a sucker, aren't ya?" he asked, as he towered over my bent and aching form.

"I need it for energy," I replied, thinking how much I'd like to attack his little girl with my hoe.

"I don't know why you need energy," he said contemptuously, "ya ain't doin' any work!"

Humiliation. Dehumanization. This work was incredibly difficult. Pay was lousy. He didn't even supply us with drinking water, he didn't care that we were hurt, and now he rubbed my nose in my miserable situation just a little more by discrediting what I had worked to accomplish in his field. I had worked harder than I had ever worked in my life to block a few rows of sugar beets so that he could eventually harvest the crop and earn a good living. Chop-rip. Chop-rip. Would the lunch break never arrive?

We found a little patch of shade and spread out blankets we had brought. Lunch conversation was sparse as we wolfed down every crumb of food and tried to grab a short nap. But our break gave us little respite. Afternoon work was even worse with the sun high and temperatures soaring. Thank goodness for those swimsuits.

More chops, more rips, more blisters. Dirt flew up our noses, in our hair, and in our eyes. More angry Mexicans drove by, honking horns. I conceded that they probably had an honest bone to pick with this particular farmer. They had a right to be angry with this guy, and to make matters worse, we had taken away their bargaining leverage by being willing to work under his unreasonable terms. I consoled myself with the conviction that at least my tan would be the best I'd ever had.

After we finally laid down our hoes and loaded our weary bones into her car at 5 o'clock, our driver managed to get us back to our houses. Exhausted, Sue and I practically crawled up to our front door. After showering and scrubbing dirt that wouldn't go away, I put medicine on my blisters and shampooed my hair twice. Finally, when I got back to my room, I looked in the mirror and saw a color I had never seen on my skin before--scarlet. On all places that my swimsuit top had not covered, my skin was sunburned a deep, serious red. I hadn't noticed it in the field, but my oiled skin had been on slow bake all day.

My mother and sister were visiting my grandmother in Mankato. In a rare show of generosity, my dad offered to take Sue and me out to dinner that night, since it was obvious that we were in no shape to cook a meal. We had to turn down his offer and send him out to Gold's Grill by himself because although we were famished and dehydrated, we were too exhausted to get up and go out.

By 7 o'clock I was asleep, but by 9 I awoke with nausea and pain. A day's exposure to sun and hard labor had produced harsh effects. My back, arms, face and thighs were blistering, and my bones and muscles ached. When I went into Sue's room, I saw that she was in the same boat.

We hobbled downstairs and drank cool water and took aspirin, but we didn't know what to do to alleviate sunburn pain. We had never before been burned, and had no ointments.

We called Mom in Mankato, and she suggested we put vinegar on our burns. Obviously she had no sunburn experience either, because the vinegar hurt like crazy. By this time we were feverish, and too timid to alert my sleeping dad. We finally put cool wet rags on our burns and waited for the aspirin to kick in.

By the time I got back to bed, around midnight, I was weeping with fatigue, but the sunburn hurt so badly that I couldn't lie down. When I finally conked out, the phone rang and my dad answered it. The caller was the driver from the previous day, and she wanted to know if I could drive today.

Taking the phone and holding it up to the ear that wasn't burnt, I explained that not only would I not drive today, but that I would not be pursuing a career in the field of beet blocking. I quit. I returned to bed, where I stayed for a couple of days. When my mother returned late Friday, I was starting to feel human again, and my skin was beginning to peel.

Apparently some of the other girls continued working for a while because a few days later one of them stopped at our house and gave both Sue and me a white envelope containing wages--I got $4.35. I guess I blocked ten rows--including the first row that I got paid less for--two miles of sugar beets. Subtracting break time, I worked about twelve hours those two days I spent as a migrant worker.

I've worked thousands of hours at various jobs throughout my life, but none stand out in my memory as vividly as those twelve terrible hours in that sugar beet field. Part of my misery was caused by the nature of the job, part by my own stupidity, but part was the uncaring and exploitative nature of the man who used me to get his work done.

Later that summer, I got a job typing for the United Fund, a job that demanded spelling and clerical skills rather than physical tolerance.

In time, after my burns and blisters healed, I had a new attitude toward those thousands of Mexican kids who traveled all the way from Texas with their families every year and who had no other options but to work day after day for lousy pay in those sugar beet fields. They must have enjoyed coming into town to see Saturday night movies. They worked unbelievably hard and deserved a lot more respect than we gave them.

Having walked a couple of miles in their shoes--up and down the rows of sugar beets-- I appreciate the plight of those migrant workers. And after listening to this story, my sophomore English students always turned back to Steinbeck's story with a little more respect for the Joads.

A Glorious Mystery
by Joan Claire Graham

"The Best Christmas Pageant Ever," a story by Barbara Robinson, tells about a family of ragtag kids who try the patience of a director and threaten to ruin the Sunday School holiday theatrical extravaganza. Robinson's story has been so successfully immortalized on the page, in film and on the stage that I could not use her title, but if I could have, I would definitely have called this story "The Best Christmas Pageant Ever."

When post World War II baby boomers entered first grade, old St. Theodore's School in Albert Lea became too small to accommodate grades 1 through 8. Under the leadership of Monsignor Bernard P. Mangan, the parish purchased land on the north side of town and made plans to expand the Catholic school. The new property was so large that ultimate expansion of the new school to include a high school was possible and probable.

The new building opened in 1954. Since that year had been designated by Pope Pius XII as a Marian Year, the powers that be at St. Theodore's parish shunned the idea of naming the school St. Theodore's Junior High or St. Theodore's Upper Campus, and decided instead to confuse everyone by naming the school St. Mary's. Schools by that name already existed in nearby towns, adding to the confusion.

Inside the front door was a little alcove with a pretty statue of Mary, and the school colors were blue and white in her honor. In its first year, St. Mary's School accommodated grades 6-9, and the lower grades stayed at St. Theodore's on Clark Street. Children from both schools attended mass at St. Theodore's Church, and then a young priest driving one 42 passenger bus ferried as many kids as possible from the church to the new school on Hawthorne and Garfield--sometimes making several trips. Having two campuses was a hassle, but the benefits of a brand new school far outweighed the drawbacks.

St. Mary's was a perfect model of 50's school architecture with its yellow stone exterior, natural light, tile floors and blond woodwork. St. Theodore grads, accustomed to old wooden desks fastened to waxed wooden floors, found new freedom to move individual formica-top tables and chairs into various group arrangements. St. Mary's students usually stayed in one classroom, but they moved to specially equipped rooms for music and science. The outdoor recreation area was large enough to field many games simultaneously. Lockers replaced cloak rooms, and parents helped a cook serve hot lunches from the fully equipped modern kitchen.

The best and most extravagant feature of the new school was the gymnasium with locker rooms, bleachers, and a stage at the end. Not only could this school field a basketball team, it provided a venue for carnivals, concerts, talent shows, and plays. The possibilities were endless.

My mother was president of the Rosary Society, the parish organization for women who supported school and church activities. In Mom's younger days, she spent a glorious year in show business working for Universal Producing Company, which owned the rights to a play called "Corporal Eagan." Universal hired young directors like my mother to go from town to town, organize a cast from among local residents, spend a modest amount of time rehearsing, and perform the show one time. Their philosophy was that if as many people as possible appeared onstage--in any capacity whatsoever-- cast members would sell tickets to everyone they knew, ensuring a full and enthusiastic house-- a great fund-raiser and morale booster for the town. Troops of scouts carried flags, choirs sang, the piano teacher accompanied, and everyone got into the act.

Remembering the glory and fun of "Corporal Eagan," Mother proposed that the new auditorium at St. Mary's be used for an annual all-school play that included every child in grades 1 through 9. Their parents would fill folding chairs and bleachers, and their enthusiastic support would help build a sense of community while giving the children experience in music, art and drama. This idea appealed to the Franciscan nuns, and Monsignor Mangan, who was normally a spoil-sport, went for the idea because he needed cash to pay for the bleachers. It appealed to the kids who had endured stark, cold, no-frills years at St. Theodore's. I can't believe how quickly the project moved forward.

Someone decided that the annual pageant would take place right before Christmas, which made a lot of sense at a Catholic school. But because of the Marian year, the director decided that the first all-school play would not be a Christmas pageant but instead would be a tribute to Mary, "The Miracle at Fatima."

For those not familiar with Catholic lore, this story is a bit on the heavy side for child actors and for audiences who expect to see a typical children's Christmas pageant. It is a true story about three Portuguese children who saw a vision of Mary in 1917 while they were herding sheep. Mary appeared several times and told the children to pray the rosary. She gave them a graphic vision of souls in hell, predicted the early death of one of the children, and warned them about World War II. As proof that the children were not lying or hallucinating about Mary, in the presence of 70,000 spectators, the sun miraculously turned silver and spun around in the sky for twelve minutes.

It would be a modern miracle for any director to pull this dramatization off on a simple stage with 250 actors aged 6-15. Even after the roles of the three children, their parents, some doubting townsfolk and the Blessed Virgin were cast, 240 kids still needed to be worked into the fabric of the play, and the stage would not hold them all during the big finale with the sun. What would an enterprising director do with all those kids who must at least have a minute on stage so that their parents would buy tickets to pay for the bleachers?

The answer lay in one of Mary's pronouncements--pray the rosary. Someone hit on the idea of forming a human rosary with younger children as rosary beads. Now that I think of it, our human rosary must have been a reenactment of a previous human rosary enacted somewhere else, because costumes arrived in the mail one day. You don't buy rosary bead costumes off a rack. Nobody has that kind of thing just lying around.

Each child had to pay a quarter to rent a costume. What does a rosary bead wear? A short satin cape and matching beanie--purple for Sorrowful Mysteries, red for Joyous Mysteries and gold for Glorious Mysteries. Girls wore Holy Communion or May Crowning white dresses, and boys wore white shirts and dark pants under their bead costumes.

Even devout Catholics have a heck of a time remembering the Mysteries of the Rosary. But when you prayed the rosary on certain days of the week, you recited the Glorious Mysteries, and on other days you recited the Joyous or Sorrowful Mysteries--one mystery before each of five decades of Hail Marys. The Joyous Mysteries were events like the

Birth of Jesus. Sorrowful Mysteries included the Crucifixion, and Glorious Mysteries included the Assumption of Mary into Heaven. You had to be Catholic to figure any of this stuff out, and even then it was chancy.

Rehearsals for "Miracle at Fatima" began in early November. I was cast as one of the five rosary beads at the front of the string--up near the cross, which was carried by an older boy. I got my job as one of the lead beads because I could carry a tune. The tune was a simplified and never before heard version of "Ave Maria." I wore a gold costume because after all the others were assigned, there were some gold ones left over. What a Glorious Mystery I was up there at the front of all three human rosaries who, one after another, assembled behind me.

The lead beads remained on stage for the entire act, while the other beads shuffled off after one "Ave Maria" to make room for the next team of Mysteries. There were fifty-five beads in each rosary, and three rosaries, so that pretty much took care of the kids in the lower school.

After Thanksgiving, we abandoned all our academics and concentrated on getting this show on the boards. The yellow school bus hauled younger kids out to St. Mary's, where we spent our entire day in the gym, either rehearsing our parts or watching the play and waiting to go onstage.

I absolutely loved the story of Jacinta, Francisco and Lucia, who talked to Mary out in the field. I envied the children who played these roles and admired the girl who played Mary. I also envied the older kids who got to do folk dances and songs within the context of the story. I hated the townspeople who didn't believe the children. I fought back tears every time Francisco died on his tiny cot.

When Mary told the children, "Pray the rosary," I eagerly stood at my post and did my best to become the best human rosary bead I could be. The human rosary scene eventually flowed flawlessly.

I memorized the entire play and recited it to my flabbergasted mother one night when she asked me about the show, and I took my responsibility as a lead bead very seriously. I eagerly anticipated the performance and excitedly counted down the days.

On the night of the performance, the nuns enforced rigid traffic and noise control and stuffed all us little rosary beads into classrooms far away from the stage. Main characters used the locker rooms on either side of the stage for dressing rooms, but those of us in the ensemble were not allowed near the gym.

No childish shrieks or peeks from curtains would rob this pageant of the dignity it deserved. Parents helped fasten our beanies and capes, and then they joined the astonished audience as the Miracle unfolded onstage and we lead beads read stories aloud to keep the other beads in line. Finally a stage manager signaled our cue and we reverently and quietly processed down the hall and approached the auditorium, which looked and sounded much different filled with spectators.

"Pray the rosary," intoned the Blessed Virgin, and as if by magic, there appeared in the aisles--and then on stage--a human musical rosary--and then another--and another! Joyous! Sorrowful! Glorious!

From the point of view of the audience sitting on a flat floor in folding chairs, each human rosary must have looked like a lot of little kids in capes and beanies circled around a boy holding a cross on a stick and singing "Ave Maria" to a tune nobody had ever heard. But I thought it was glorious. I felt thrilled and important to be a part of such an awe-inspiring extravaganza. How proud my parents must have been to see my caped and beanied back through three complete human rosaries!

At the end of the play, after the sun had stopped spinning and both the townsfolk in the play and the parents in the audience were convinced that a miracle had indeed taken place, the entire cast crowded the stage and part of the bleachers for the finale and sang all three verses of "Hail Holy Queen Enthroned Above."

"Miracle at Fatima" was so successful that an all-school pageant was performed for several years. The next year the director chose a show more traditionally associated with Christmas, "No Room in the Inn."

Our rehearsal schedule remained the same year after year. During December,we produced a play. We didn't do math, science, or catechism.

We sang, we danced, we learned lines and we cooperated. Some of us fell in love with the process of pulling together so many elements into one beautiful experience. I moved up from rosary bead to play several singing angels, a dancing ice skater, various members of ensembles, and an angel in a tableau. Mothers sewed angel gowns and skating skirts, but fancier costumes came from somewhere else.

Elaborate costumes for wise men and shepherds were hauled out of trunks each year. I don't know where they came from. Maybe the nuns made them during summers. Spotlights and gels were borrowed or rented, musical accompanists were brought in, and Tony Zimmney, a carpenter whose many children attended the school, supervised construction of beautiful, professional looking sets. Some of our nuns might have written the plays and music, because all the material, except for traditional carols, was original. Our pageants gave many people an outlet for creativity and a sense of accomplishment, but after six years, a new principal arrived and the Christmas Pageant was discontinued.

St. Mary's never expanded into a high school. After tearing down the old school, building a new St. Theodore's on the east side of the church, adding classrooms and a convent at St. Mary's, and building a new rectory, the parish suffered declining enrollment and a scarcity of teaching nuns. Eventually both schools closed. St. Theodore's reopened in the 90's and is thriving as an elementary school, but St. Mary's was sold to Thorncrest, an assisted living facility for the elderly.

I visited Thorncrest recently and tried to figure out where the rooms of St. Mary's had been. As near as I could figure, the gym and stage are now Thorncrest's dining hall and kitchen. Though I tried to explain to the social director how wonderful those Christmas pageants were in that room nearly fifty years ago, I couldn't quite capture the magic for someone who had not seen the building in its original configuration.

The Christmas pageants were always first rate. How the nuns produced them year after year was another glorious mystery. Cast members and parents pitched in, did their best, and felt proud to be involved. Most of the kids had lot of fun and gained important arts experience. I'll bet those shows were the Best Christmas Pageants Ever, but that title has already been used by another writer.

Trading Stamps and the Road to Redemption
by Steve Swanson

Merchants had never found a gimmick half so powerful: trading stamps. Gold Bond, one of the most successful and popular trading stamps, was founded by Minnesota's own Curt Carlson. With a $55 loan from his landlord, Carlson started a business that evolved into a multi-billion dollar empire. Most of us didn't pay much attention to Carlson's empire, but we became obsessed with trading stamps.

Carlson enlisted Anfin Odland's grocery store in south Minneapolis as the first business to offer Gold Bond stamps in 1938. Customers, who received ten stamps for each dollar spent, pasted stamps into a little book and redeemed a full book for $3. Books contained 24 pages that held 50 stamps, so a filled book represented an expenditure of $120. During the Depression, a $3 rebate was a great incentive to shop at Odland's.

The Gold Bond company grew steadily until 1953, when Carlson landed the Super Value account. In nine months, the stamps boosted Super Value's sales by 63 percent. With working capital at last, and at the urging of Super Value, Carlson made a line of premiums available to stamp savers through mail order catalogs and Redemption Centers.

Trading stamp frenzy ensued. Some stores gave Green Stamps, others gave Gold Bond, Gift Bond, or other kinds. Erickson's gas station gave stamps redeemable for dishes displayed in showcases right at the pumps. Raleigh cigarettes printed stamps on packs, and a smoker with a cough made a morose joke about redeeming Raleigh stamps for an iron lung. Betty Crocker put a slight twist on the stamp act with coupons redeemable for flatware and cook books.

Everyone saved stamps. I remember a blasphemous cartoon at the time, "Jesus Saves--Gold Bond Stamps." The Smothers Brothers sang a parody of "Greensleeves" called " Green Stamps." Stamps became a ubiquitous part of popular culture. Smaller and more plentiful than postage stamps, trading stamps came in both sheets and strips. A large supermarket purchase would net the shopper a two foot streamer of stamps from a thumb-operated machine by the register.

On boring nights shoppers could lick themselves spitless pasting stamps carefully (mind the printed grid) into passport-sized books. Green Stamp books were Scotch plaid, Gold Bond books featured Sandy Saver, a winking little cartoon Scotsman, on the cover. Books, which started neat but got fat and cumbersome as pages filled and glue stiffened, were commonly kept by savers in shoe boxes.

Redemption Centers cropped up in department stores and offices, where handsomely displayed premiums offered further incentives to save stamps. Premiums, ranging from trivial to huge, represented stuff the average shopper would like to have without spending money. Although merchants factored the cost of stamps into the price of merchandise, stores didn't usually offer a discount to shoppers who didn't want stamps.

Stamp savers perused catalogs at home so they could plan their visits to Redemption Centers. Pinking shears, toys, card tables, can openers, egg beaters, pans, baking dishes and alarm clocks cost anywhere from a half book to three books. The most popular items at the Gold Bond Redemption Centers were steam irons, Hamilton wrist watches, sheets and pillow cases.

Friends sometimes swapped Green Stamps for Gold Bond to maximize their redemption power. The most expensive item in Gold Bond's 1963 line was a Maytag washer for 109 books. If a shopper spent $13,080 at a store that gave stamps, she could redeem those stamps for a free washer. The average income was $5600, a new car cost $2300, and a gallon of gas cost a quarter, so collecting 109 books of trading stamps took a lot of spending and a lot of spit. Rather than buy a Maytag washing machine for $200 and redeem the stamps from its purchase for an egg beater, a stamp saver could redeem all her stamps from the purchase of five and a half new cars to get a washer!

Stamps were the only acceptable currency at Redemption Centers. If a shopper came up a few stamps short, she was not allowed to supplement cash to get the desired item. Redemption Center personnel checked and double checked to make sure all books had 24 pages and all pages contained fifty stamps. Books could be traded in whole or ripped into quarters or halves because some items cost three and a half books or nine and three quarters books.

By 1960, Gold Bond employed 700 and ran 200 stores and grossed $50 million. By 1966, their peak year, they did $200 million worth of business. During this frenzy, when every business gave some kind of trading stamps, and thousands of Minnesota families spent countless hours licking, sticking, planning, and redeeming, the bottom fell out of the trading stamp business. One savvy store lured customers by offering lower prices without stamps, and within a few years stamps became passe.

The whole trading stamp phenomenon sounds like one of John Calvin's 15th Century sermon illustrations--irresistible grace, a valuable little book, free gifts--Redemption Centers. Stamps were rewarded like Sunday school attendance stickers or grade school gold stars. Trading stamps paved the way for other customer loyalty incentives like frequent flyer miles and grocery discount cards.

My wife tells me we still have a 40-year-old French casserole and a Stanley thermos that we redeemed stamps to get. She thinks some businesses still give stamps. With today's inflation, stamps must be cumbersome. Imagine a person licking herself or himself dead dry after buying new kitchen appliances, hors d'oeuvres for a wedding, or a computer. I suppose stamps today are self -adhesive, but it doesn't seem that saving them like we once did would fit into today's lifestyle.

Steve Swanson is an author, a retired English professor and a member of the Lutheran clergy. He writes a column "Now and then" for the Northfield Daily news.

Smaller and more plentiful than postage stamps, trading stamps came in both sheets and strips. A large supermarket purchase would net the shopper a two foot streamer of stamps from a thumb-operated machine by the register.

Armistice Day Storm in Milaca
by Lloyd Deuel

My father, Ira Deuel, started in the school bus business in the fall of 1938. He and my mother had bought a restaurant tavern at Foreston in 1937, and in one year had enough capital (about $200) to buy a used school bus. A bus was needed to transport high school kids from the Foreston community to Milaca High School. This was in the midst of the Great Depression, and few men could come up with that amount of money.

This school bus, found near Deerwood, was a three-seater with two bench seats with backs running the length of the bus on each side and one seat running down the center of the bus. The girls sat on the outside facing in, and the boys straddled the middle seat facing towards the front. There was no criticism of this arrangement because just a few years prior there had been no bus service between Foreston and Milaca. The big comment was the ugly color--a two-tone tan and brown that left a lot to be desired even back then.

This old Studebaker started to wear out. My dad figured the economics and decided that if he could expand his districts to include District 8, 6, 7, and Lincoln District, as well as part of others under contract, he could swing a deal to buy a new 48 passenger bus. Each country school district paid my dad for each kid he hauled for them, but the high school did not compensate him.

My dad got his new Ford school bus from Ed Odegard, the Ford dealer in Milaca just in time for the 1940 school year. He paid $2,200 for this beauty. This was still Depression time, and there were those who offered the opinion that he wouldn't live long enough to finish payments on it and I, his son, would have to make them.

My dad was very proud of his new bus. He had an exceptionally loud voice that his hunting dogs, horses, high school kid riders and I were very much aware of. Before each school year, he would give a lecture to the bus full of kids that this was his bus, and he didn't want to find any -- whatever they called it before the term "graffiti" became popular-- on his bus. He had other rules that sometimes seemed to go on and on.

Armistice Day, November 11, 1940, fell on a Monday. Foreston Grade School observed the holiday, but Milaca High School did not, meaning that the big kids had to go to school but the little kids didn't. I was in fifth grade and thought this was really neat.

The day started with a light rain, but when the bus loaded up in Foreston, a few snowflakes started to appear. By the time my dad unloaded at the school, which was 3 miles distant on Highway 23, the visibility was very limited and blizzard was imminent, in my dad's opinion. He found the school superintendent nearby when the bus unloaded and suggested taking the kids back home at that time. A turf dispute developed over who outranked who, school superintendent or bus owner/ operator. My dad went back to Foreston without the kids.

As my dad walked in the door at home, I answered the telephone, and it was the school secretary asking me to inform my dad that school had been canceled for the bus kids and he should come and get them. By this time, it was really getting nasty outside, and my dad asked my mom to get out his winter clothes so he could change clothes when he got back from Milaca and before he tackled the country roads. Since it had been nice in the early morning, neither he nor most of the kids wore jackets, headgear, gloves or boots when they started for school. My dad planned to gas up his bus too when he returned from Milaca. These were two quick miscalculations he made.

Visibility was bad when Dad returned to Milaca, and cars had run off the road. He loaded the kids and started back to Foreston on a good paved road, which should have been an easy three miles. He got exactly half way when he had to stop for cars that were stuck in a huge snow bank that formed in a cut in the road bank. Cars following the bus got hung up so that Dad couldn't back up.

He left the bus and waded through snow about 100 yards back towards Milaca to a driveway of a farmhouse, then another 100 yards south to the house. An elderly couple, Mr. and Mrs. Nelson, lived there, and they had a telephone.

Dad first called the state highway department, and then he called the county highway department to ask for help. The county had bought very few good snowplows for county roads during the Depression, and villages and townships had no money for snowplowing. School bus travel was limited to county roads and state highways during winter. After some jurisdiction questions were settled, Dad was promised help, which turned out to be four county snowplows that got stuck behind cars that were stuck like his bus. By afternoon Dad realized that there would be no help from either the county or the state, and he had 33 kids on his bus.

He called home and gave my mother some names of men who might be available to help him and asked her to call them. He then walked to Foreston to figure out what to do. By this time, the snow was wet and getting deep, and the wind was blowing strong. Surprisingly, the temperature was not very cold. The Nelsons had loaned him a jacket, gloves, and a towel to wrap around his head, and he looked like a walking snowman.

The men who showed up to help him on the first afternoon were Harry Kruger, Hugh Amo, Jack Buisman, Ted Frazier, and Earl DeHart. They were all strong, well-dressed for the weather, and in the prime of their lives. They decided to bring gasoline for the bus on a toboggan because they felt the bus should be kept running. Also, my dad was to call the Nelsons for their input on the feasibility of bringing kids to their house for the night.

The safety of 33 kids was beginning to weigh pretty heavily on my dad by this time. He thought about the instructions he had left with them: leave a couple windows cracked, open the door and turn off the engine every 20 minutes, monitor everyone for signs of sleepiness, and stay in the bus. He said afterwards that he thought of more things he should have added.

There was a house on the north side of Highway 23 about a mile and a half from Foreston and about a fourth mile from the bus, where Reverend and Mrs. Stone lived. The men had pulled the toboggan this far and needed a rest. The Stones had a very small house but offered hospitality for a couple of kids if need be. The weather had turned colder and snow was not wet, but it felt like sleet when it hit bare flesh. Two boys, Lawrence Thome and Howard Vallencourt, went to the Stones' house and ended up staying with them until Friday.

The kids were all okay, and my dad explained the plan to them. My dad would lead the way to the Nelson house, and they would all hold hands and go together in one long chain. The other men would be interspersed in the chain with two men bringing up the rear.

When the kids left the bus, the shock of the storm took their breath away. The chain rule was immediately broken when kids ran back for the warmth of the bus. It was so cold for the kids, without winter clothing, that some of them just lay down and gave up. The men started dragging kids in the path made by my dad and the one kid he held on to. When he reached the Nelsons' door, Dad pushed the kid in and went back for more kids. He met some of the men coming with kids, and he sidestepped to go help others.

Back at the bus, Harry Kruger pulled and pushed kids out the back door while Jack Buisman stood on the outside and pulled kids through the door and prevented others from getting back into the bus. They both said later they would never forget this terrible experience, and they needed more help for their task. It was completely dark when Kruger and Buisman left the bus and brought up the rear on their way to the Nelson house.

They were totally exhausted, but they couldn't rest until a head count of the 31 kids came out right, and counting was hard to do. The house was pretty big, two stories, and lots of rooms. Thirty-one kids all scattered were hard to count, but the count was finally determined to be correct.

The men left the house and headed back to the bus to check if anything had been lost. Also, responsibility weighed heavily on all of them, and they were not comfortable with the head count.

They paused when the path seemed covered, and one man noticed they were standing on top of a car. They hadn't noticed this car before, so they dug down to check inside. A young mother in the car with her two young children said they were waiting for a wrecker to come and pull her car out of the snow bank. The men convinced her that there would be no wrecker and that she should come with them to the Nelsons'. They then led her and carried the little kids to safety.

They said later that it was luck that they found that family because no other people came by that night or until later the next day. The mother and her children would not have survived.

The new head count for the Nelson house was now 34. The Nelsons had food, but not for that many unexpected guests, so my dad promised to bring more supplies the next day. My dad gave another lecture and set of instructions for the kids on how to act for the Nelsons, and the men started the walk to the Stone house.

By this time it was getting colder, still snowing and blowing, and visibility was so bad they almost missed the Stone house-even with the yard lights on. After a brief rest at the Stones', the men had a hard, long, mile walk back to Foreston. Their outer clothes were frozen so that they had to have help to even sit down. They were utterly exhausted.

Our telephone had been ringing continuously all afternoon and evening, and it was my job to inform everyone (parents, relatives, friends, even the superintendent) as to the status of the school bus kids. This was pretty heady stuff for someone who normally wouldn't have such responsibility.

The next morning the storm hadn't abated, and the new snow-drifts were pretty awesome. My dad called Mrs. Nelson for her grocery list. Besides flour, pancake syrup, coffee (high school kids drank coffee back then) and sugar, she wanted flashlight batteries. It seems she had no problem offering hospitality, but she wasn't about to allow any hanky-panky (her words) in her house, so she sat up all night with her flashlight to monitor the kids.

My dad got a crew of men together, and they carried bags full of groceries to the Nelson house. There were no snowplows, cars, or train traffic that day.

When the men reached the school bus, they found the drifts were level with the top of the bus. The snow had sucked around the bus so that there was bare blacktop for about 4 feet around it. The interior of his new bus, however, was packed with snow.

The kids were all okay, and Mrs. Nelson had no problems. Mr. Nelson happily reported that the farm boys volunteered to help him with chores that morning, and he had never had such good help. Most kids had called home or gotten word to their families that they were fine. In 1940 there were still homes with no telephone service or electricity. The Nelsons had both--and even a radio.

By Tuesday afternoon, snow had drifted on the north end of Main Street in Foreston so that if one stood on either sidewalk, the tops of the buildings across the street were barely visible. Snow still fell and blew, and the temperature fell to about 0 degrees. Windchill wasn't computed in those days, but it would have been awesome. It was reported that farmers had a terrible time getting their livestock under shelter, but they fared better than expected. Snowplowed country roads were scarce in 1940, and horses and sleds were still the old standbys.

On Wednesday morning the Foreston Main Street snow bank was even with the top of the buildings. The temperature was colder, but the old timers said that if it got just a little bit colder, it would be too cold to keep snowing. That wasn't to happen until Friday.

On Wednesday a rotary snowplow, (the first I ever saw), came from St. Cloud and broke through the snowdrifts nearly to where the bus was. It had to stop before it got to the bus because of all the cars blocking the road in front of the bus.

My dad got his buddies and other men with cars and trucks and made it to the Petersons' house. They started the slow process of getting the kids to the vehicles and then on to Foreston. By late afternoon, all the kids were in town. The country kids either stayed with friends in town or were taken home by their families by horse and sled if they didn't live too far from town.

On Thursday the blizzard seemed worse, and there was no snow-plow activity. My dad and the men took a well-earned rest that day.

On Friday morning it was a lot colder, and they said it was not snowing, but I couldn't tell the difference because the wind was drifting the snow so much. The train came through with a huge snowplow and got train traffic moving, and a highway plow came from St. Cloud.

The only way to get around Foreston by this time was on skis. The Foreston Main Street and two other short streets were not to be plowed out until Christmas week. There was no school for the Foreston Grade School kids because the teachers had gone home for the three-day weekend, and all the roads were closed and they couldn't get back.

The St. Cloud snowplow came through on Highway 23 to plow to Milaca, but couldn't get past my dad's bus. They had to tow the bus all the way back to Foreston to get around it. My dad got the bus pushed into our heated garage, and it became my job to shovel snow out of the inside because I was small enough to do it standing up. It took me nearly the whole weekend.

On Monday morning, my dad's route was shortened to staying on Highway 23 as none of the other roads were plowed. Most of the kids were ready for school again, but they were surely dressed differently than the week before. My dad contacted most of the parents and kids over the weekend, and none reported any sickness or ill effects.

Customers Have to Detour to Milaca Stores --- Cause of Tieup on Highway 169 Monday --- Snow Drifts Are Over Eight Feet High

MILLE LACS COUNTY TIMES
Leading County Newspaper---10,500 Readers

WO DEAD IN COUNTY IN WORST BLIZZARD IN STATE'S HISTORY

One result of this ordeal was that the kids and my dad developed closeness or bonding that lasted the rest of their lives. That Christmas the kids, my dad, and some of the parents took up a collection and gave a meaningful Christmas present to the Nelsons in appreciation for their hospitality. At the end of the school term, my dad took the bus load of kids (I got to go along) up to Shore Acres on Mille Lacs Lake for a picnic. He continued this activity every year until gas rationing curtailed it during World War II.

Another aftermath of this near-catastrophe was that the superintendent and the one who followed him always called my dad early in the morning on bad weather days to ask him about the weather out there in the country.

My dad was always truthful, and if he suggested it was too bad to go out on the roads, the school day would immediately be canceled. Dad's school bus lasted 17 full school terms, which must be some kind of record for longevity.

Lloyd Deuel is a retired machinist who lives with his wife Phyllis in Brooklyn Center. They enjoy gardening, woodworking and retirement.

Paper Route Years 1943-47
by Lloyd Deuel

I graduated from the eighth grade of District 11 in Foreston in the spring of 1943. My best friend and classmate, Chuck DeHart, got a job candling eggs for Floyd Clark in his produce business, so Chuck turned over his daily paper route to me.

Three evening daily papers and one morning paper were delivered in Foreston at that time. Nearly every family in this town of 300 subscribed to a newspaper of one kind or another. I delivered the Evening Tribune and the Evening Journal and Morning Tribune. Another kid had the Evening Star. When these papers went through a merger, the other kid quit his route and I had all of them.

I delivered about 45 daily papers and about 135 Sunday papers. This was a lot of work, but there were benefits. I learned responsibility, record keeping, and customer relations in a very short time, and Chuck and I had more spending money than most kids in town.

It took well over an hour to deliver papers in summer when I could ride my bike. In winter and spring when it wasn't bike weather, delivery took much longer. The Sunday paper route was much larger and more time consuming. There was also the dog problem. My spaniel usually went with me, and it seemed every dog in town confronted him or vice-versa. If the other dog was bigger and I was on my bike, my dog kept the bike between them, and both dogs made lots of noise.

One day my dog wasn't along, and after I threw the paper on a customer's front porch, their collie attacked me. He bit my leg and pulled me down, and when I was on my back, he let go and went for my face. I threw up my left arm, and he clamped down and started to drag me back towards the house. I was big for 14 years old, but this dog was big too.

The customer, Roy Hall, and his schoolteacher daughter came running out of their house when they heard my screams. By the time they got the dog to let go, I was bleeding from both my arm and leg. They called my mother, and she drove to the scene.

In the meantime, an old man who lived next door, Mr. Thelander, came over to offer his expertise. His opinion was to rub salt on the bites to sanitize the wounds. I heard this advice about six times before someone decided to take me to the doctor for sutures. This caused even more concern because I had been bitten by a German Shepherd the year before, and I knew all about stitches.

Dr. Kling decided I needed sutures two places on my arm and the long tear on my leg. After stitching, he wrapped wax paper around the wounds to delay healing and made impressive bandages. The plus side of this experience was showing kids my neat arm sutures, but the negative side was I couldn't drop my pants to show my leg wounds.

Doctor Kling couldn't remember my dog bites from the year before because treating a dog bite was quite common in those days, but he did remember my mother paying the $2 bill, as prompt bill payment was not common. As for the dogs in both cases, they were severely beaten by their owners. I don't remember if the Halls offered to pay my doctor bill. The doctor advised checking the dog for signs of rabies, but there wasn't much of that going around in those days.

Not all paper route problems involved dogs. Snowplowed streets in Foreston did not exist in the mid 1940's, so walking the paper route was really tough. My dad had bought Alaskan snowshoes for each of us for fox hunting, and I soon became adept and used them to deliver papers. It was still cold and dark when I finished, but using snowshoes tends to keep one warm.

In the late winter of 1944, my dad bought me a horse for $35. He was a pretty chestnut horse that weighed a little over 900 pounds. His name was Rusty, and my dad and I had to break him for riding. Rusty loved to run. He had only three gaits: walk, trot, and gallop. Rusty was in full gallop as soon as my right foot reached the stirrup after mounting, and he could pivot at full gallop.

My dad, who was a good carpenter, built a 12'x16' stable for Rusty with a second floor for hay. Whether I rode him or not, I had to feed, water, and clean Rusty's stall twice a day. I really didn't mind this, as he was my horse.

Rusty soon learned the paper route as well as I and would turn into the customer's walkway, walk up the steps and onto the porch. I would lean down from the saddle and put the paper in the screen door. I could deliver the whole route without getting out of the saddle. Only when I saw a customer downtown and gave him his paper would there be a problem. Rusty didn't know the customer already had his paper. When we arrived at the customer's house, Rusty would turn in on his own, catching me unaware, and I had to be a good rider to stay in the saddle. Rusty and I were a team, and we had this routine down so well we could deliver the route in about 35 minutes.

Both my parents grew up in Foreston, and it seemed I was related to everyone in town. Since I had no brothers or sisters, my relatives thought it was a handicap for me not to have a sister to snitch on me. They took it on themselves to help out. To me, their snitch patrol seemed immense.

Frank Dilly remarked that when I came to his house I would jump Rusty onto his porch, slide up to his door, put the paper in the screen door, and jump Rusty off the porch. He claimed he would no longer stand in back of his door because he could envision Rusty and me crashing through it. When this reached my parents via snitch patrol, my dad gave me instructions to rein in my horse before I reached the steps, walk him up the steps, turn him around not pivoting, and walk him back down the steps.

Most of the houses in Foreston had big wooden porches with wooden steps. My customers started getting nervous about a horse walking up the steps and across the porch. One by one they requested me to deliver the paper to the back porch. where the steps were concrete. This was no big deal for me because how long does it take for a running horse to reach the back door?

When winter came and Foreston streets turned to hard packed snow, ruts, and ice, my dad decided Rusty needed to be sharp shod. My dad had worked as an apprentice blacksmith in his younger day and was an excellent horse shoer. He fitted horseshoes with hardened tapered steel cleats like the cleats on football shoes. Rusty got used to these very quickly and soon discovered that he could start, stop, and turn quicker than before. I used to say that he could pivot on a dime, but now he could leave change too and leave me floating through the air like a dollar bill.

One Saturday afternoon after I saddled up Rusty, the fire whistle blew. I was a Foreston volunteer fireman, so I tied Rusty outside and answered the call. The fire didn't amount to much so I was back in a couple hours to do the paper route, but I forgot to tighten the saddle cinch. When I leaned over to drop the paper in Art Enius's door, the saddle turned bottom side up. I clung to the saddle for quite awhile because I was afraid to let go. All I could see were those sharp shod hooves on my bucking horse from under his belly. Normally Rusty couldn't buck me off, but when he discovered this opportunity, he couldn't resist. On this nice Saturday winter afternoon I think most of the Foreston community was standing on sidewalks in full view of the Enius yard. When Rusty finally dumped me into a big snowdrift, we really made the bystanders' day.

In winter it was usually dark before I finished the route. As we approached Highway 23 one evening, a semi truck was speeding through town without its lights on. I reined in my horse, but he cut too far to the left off the road and tried to run across the big highway ditch that was level with snow.

He sank all the way to the bottom of the ditch, and I was thrown completely across the highway spread-eagle on my stomach. Before I could get up, the truck was almost crossways in a jackknife position between Rusty and me. As the truck straightened up and went on, Rusty and I got up and continued on the route. I never talked to that truck driver, but did notice afterwards that he slowed to a crawl when driving through Foreston.

Foreston had free cowboy movies like Hopalong Cassidy on Wednesday nights during summer. In those films, riders did fancy tricks, so the kids asked me if I could learn to do some. This was nearly my undoing. Rusty and I practiced fast mounting where I would stand with both hands on the saddle horn, start Rusty in a gallop, and then swing up and over the back of the saddle.

For our other trick, we galloped full bore down Foreston Main Street, and I tilted my head back and lost my cap. Rusty pivoted so I could lean far down on the left side and pick up my cap. Both tricks required a great deal of strength from me.

The snitch patrol kicked in, and my mother let me know what she thought of my head being inches away from the gravel street. I stopped doing this trick on Main Street.

One summer Sunday morning I was delivering my papers. I had a bigger route on Sunday, and the papers were much larger, so I had to go back to replenish the bag. The Catholic Church bell was ringing so I knew I was running late. As Rusty galloped full speed down the center of Main Street going south approaching the only blind intersection in town, a Model A Ford approached that same intersection traveling west. A lady who lived on a farm near Foreston was taking her kids to church, and she was running late. Model A Fords were about 15 years old, but had no mufflers, and had mechanical brakes (no brakes). I heard her just before reaching the intersection, but she didn't see me until the last second.

As she looked up and saw horse and rider bearing down on her passenger side, I was able to lean to the left and Rusty veered enough so that my right stirrup just missed the back of her car. My thought was that I would have to slow down in the future on this intersection.

Later in the morning, the lady's husband came to town to buy a paper from me. He told me that his wife was really angry. After letting the kids off at church, she drove home, changed clothes and insisted he pick up the kids because she was too upset to drive back to town. He thought this was funny and told everyone the story, much to my consternation. Just about everyone in town, except my parents, heard the story. I kept waiting for the other shoe to drop.

When school let out in the spring of 1944, I was offered a job with the Foreston Hardware and Lumber Company working on a roofing crew. An old man, Fred Samuelson, ran the two or three man crew. Fred had the reputation of being cranky and hard to get along with. I found this was due to his being a perfectionist working with helpers who were not.

I was husky and strong for 14 nearly 15 years old and could carry bundles of shingles and roofing up the ladders with no problem. We worked 10-hour days, 6 days a week. I became the driver of our truck, a 1935 Chevrolet. Fred and I got along great and remained friends for many years after.

This company that I worked for had another truck, a 1941 Chevrolet, and in 1944 when there were no new trucks or cars built due to the war, this was a really nice truck. This truck was used for delivering lumber and used machinery, and finding drivers was a big problem. The manpower situation was acute, and soon just boys and young women drove the truck. The truck was rolled upside down, so a new driver was needed.

My dad was asked if I could be taken off the roofing crew to become the full-time truck driver. He was very reluctant, but wartime made changes necessary. My $3 a day pay remained the same as when I was a roofer. I liked the idea of being out of that hot sun and was pleased with the promotion. The day that I turned 15 and received my driver's license in the mail, I was asked to drive to the southern part of the state for a load of machinery and come back the next day. The 35 mile per hour speed limit made trips very time consuming.

I still got up early on Sunday morning to deliver my papers. I got a kick out of asking people, "How many over-the- road truck drivers deliver Sunday papers on horseback?"

When I started working on summer vacation from school, I had to hire a kid to deliver my papers. This was quite a labor relation's challenge. I could get a younger kid to deliver for a nickel a day. The downside was he wasn't old enough to read yet and couldn't handle the names on the route roster. I had to pay more for competent help, but tried to keep it under a quarter, which still allowed me some profit. When they missed a customer, he would call my parents, and when I came home from work before supper, I had to deliver the paper that my employee missed.

There was never any question about waiting until after supper because my parents always stressed dependability. This arrangement of hiring a substitute carried on every summer when I worked, as well as two falls when I went out for high school football and three springs for baseball. My customers were very understanding.

I used to quote the old mail service slogan, "Through rain, sleet, mud, or snow the mail goes through." My saying was, "By foot, snowshoe, bike, or horseback, the Minneapolis Star and Tribune will be delivered." This was intended to soften complaints.

In the winter there were many mornings when the thermometer was in the 20 to 30 degrees below zero range. By afternoon the temperature would often be in 10 to 20 below range, and the wind would be reported 20 to 35 miles per hour. I would think about delivering papers all day at school. The big decision was whether to walk or snowshoe the route and be warm or saddle up Rusty and go around the route fast and very cold. I always thought that the saddle was at least 20 degrees colder than the air.

When I graduated from high school in 1947, I had delivered papers for four full years. I had a good relationship with my representatives from the Minneapolis Star and Tribune that I dealt with. They would check with me and tell me they had no complaints from my customers, and no pep talks to try to get me to sell more papers as I had about every house in town.

I would offer to let them ride my horse, and they would be flattered but refuse. These were city guys who always wore suits and used that as an excuse. They asked a lot of questions about the horse. They also seemed to have promotions and contests going to promote more sales, which I couldn't win, so they would load me up with extra prizes like pen and pencil sets or flashlights that they had in their car.

There were other perks to having the route for so long. Mrs. Art Enius was known for her cake baking. She especially made a triple layer chocolate cake that was just out this world. Every so often she would have a huge piece on a plate with a glass of milk waiting for me. Mrs. Oscar Stromwall had a huge rhubarb bed and would can rhubarb in season. She learned that I love rhubarb and would wait for me with a bowl of fresh warm rhubarb sauce. As time went on, the bowl became a small mixing bowl.

I had other customers who would offer a napkin full of fudge or other candy. One lady made homemade root beer and would offer a huge cold mug on summer days. Generally I was always in a hurry to finish my route, but my mother taught good manners, so I would always take time to partake in my customers' generosity and thank them.

As the school year was nearing the end and I would be graduating from high school, I informed my customers that I would be turning the route over to another kid. I did this mainly so I could make the final collection at that time too. I believe it cost my customers 45 cents a week for all seven papers. I think all my customers settled their bill and gave me one dollar for a graduation gift. I was very impressed and appreciated their generosity.

For the last couple years, I had developed a bad case of sinus or hay fever. After graduating from school, I didn't ride Rusty very much, but when I did, I really suffered from hay fever. I finally figured out that I was allergic to Rusty. I could take care of him with no problem, but when I rode him and he warmed up, it was bad.

A horse needs to be worked or ridden and have attention. We decided it wasn't fair to keep Rusty. A riding academy was interested in him, as he was a gentle horse and safe for people to be around. We decided the academy would be a good home for him. Although I was ready to move on in life, I felt like I had lost a member of my family.

Growing up in an Owatonna Corner Grocery Store
by Donald Matejcek

My dad died when I was 5, so my mother had to find a way to raise my three older sisters and me in Owatonna. Within a year she was able to buy a little corner grocery store, located at Freemont and Grove. These family-run corner stores not only sold food to people in the neighborhood, but also provided them with a place to interact and exchange news about the world and their daily lives.

Matejcek Grocery Store occupied a large room on the main floor of a very small house. Behind the store our family occupied one bedroom, a living room and a kitchen. The bathroom and another bedroom were upstairs. We kept excess stock on shelves and in the aisles in the basement, and five of us lived in the remaining space.

I slept on the living room couch until we built a bedroom in the basement. About that time, a lady who worked as a bank teller moved in to help with the store and the family. This made the house even fuller, and with five women in the house, I was dead wrong five times before I even opened my mouth.

Soon after we opened for business, my sister Marilyn, who is a year and a half older than I, was diagnosed with Bulbar polio and confined to an iron lung at the Sister Kenny Hospital in Minneapolis. Fearing they would contract polio, customers stayed away from our store.

A news reporter wrote an article dispelling fears and urging people to support my mother's only source of income during this difficult time, and the Knights of Columbus encouraged members to go out of their way to make purchases at our little store. Fortunately, both the store and Marilyn made it through that tough period.

Working at the store was a fact of life that we did not question. Mom opened for business at 8 a.m. and closed at 8 p.m. six days a week. On Sundays we all took a day off. After school, during summers, and on weekends, we kids pitched in. While my sisters worked behind the counter, I did what everyone thought were boys' jobs.

By the time I was 8, I kept the pop machine stocked and hauled canned and packaged goods to and from the basement storage area. After a heavy snow, I shoveled the roof so that ice dams wouldn't form. I helped clean the store and scraped wads of gum off the sidewalk out front. Because of all that scraping, I hate gum to this day.

Our pop machine was a big chest that held ice. After putting a nickel in the slot, the buyer moved a Coke bottle along a track and through a little gate that the nickel unlocked. I had to keep pop and ice in that machine and had to drain and clean it. My worst experience came as a result of the delivery man's tendency to set pop cases out in the heat before loading bottles into that icy water. The temperature change sometimes caused pop bottles to explode, and I had to clean up a terrible mess. I finally got smart and told the delivery man to let me load the bottles after they had cooled down.

The pop machine, ice cream freezer, meat cooler and dairy case were the only cool places in the store during summer. A bell on the door jingled the arrival and departure of each customer, followed by the sound of the screen door slamming. A small fan helped keep the cashier comfortable during hot months, and of course we were allowed to eat Popsicles, Fudgesicles and Push-ups-- favorite summer treats.

Most families in those days didn't buy large quantities of ice cream or pop because home refrigerators were quite small, with freezing compartments big enough to hold only a couple of ice cube trays and a quart of ice cream. Our ice cream freezer always contained a couple of big cardboard tubs of ice cream from the dairy. We packed ice cream into pint boxes for customers to take home and eat immediately, and we also served ice cream cones. My sister liked to fill a mixing bowl with ice cream, cover it with chocolate sauce, and eat it after closing time.

Our friends envied the fact that we had access to treats whenever we wanted them, but those treats were the only payment we got for our work. I didn't earn any money until I got a paper route at age 10. Of course, I still had to go to school and work at the store, Although these responsibilities limited my free time, I was able to incorporate my professional responsibilities into my social life by supplying friends with occasional cigarettes and cigars.

Work and social life frequently overlapped. My mother was a popular confidante to many neighborhood housewives whose opportunities to get out of their houses were limited by the fact that they didn't have cars to use during the day. Most customers walked to our store and carried purchases home in paper bags. Mothers pushed baby strollers, and small children rode tricycles. Since we were located near the outskirts of town, farmers sometimes stopped on their way out of town, which added to our mix of customers and the things they talked about.

Although small, Matejcek Grocery was a full-service store that could supply customers with everything they needed. One popular product was meat for cold cuts. After a customer made a selection, the clerk hoisted a big chunk of turkey, beef loaf, or ham onto the meat saw table and sliced a few pieces. We'd weigh the order, wrap the cuts in white paper, and tie the paper with string. We got chops and other meat from a butcher shop down the street and sold a fair amount of ground beef.

Children loved to stand before our glass candy case, where cardboard boxes displayed rows of licorice whips, Lick um Aid, jaw breakers, Double Bubblegum, stick candy, caramels, malted milk balls and kisses. Baseball cards and other kinds of trading cards came in a packet with a sheet of bubble gum. For a nickel a kid could spend a lot of time looking, buy five pieces of candy, and carry home his treasure in a little brown paper bag. Another popular attraction was a gumball machine that dispensed occasional plastic charms and prizes along with gum.

I don't recall that we ever had any trouble. We never got robbed, and customers were courteous. By the mid 50's, however, large supermarkets started up-- offering low prices and fancy displays. They lured customers with newspaper ads and specials. They offered carts to help shoppers gather large quantities of groceries and carry-out boys who helped load purchases into the customer's car. It took a few years, but eventually customers began to prefer that type of grocery shopping.

Lifestyles changed too. Housewives gained mobility when their families bought second cars and freezers and big refrigerators. Customers used corner stores for convenience stops, for milk and bread, but did their big shopping elsewhere and bragged about savings and convenience. Small neighborhood grocery stores, once the hub of neighborhood commerce and activity, fell on hard times.   About this same time, our family work force began to shrink. My oldest sister married a guy in the Air Force. After staying to help Mom in the store for about a year, she moved away to attend school. My second sister moved to the Cities to work, and Marilyn got a job at the court house and then moved to Colorado.

In 1961, the year I graduated from high school, Mom sold the stock and equipment and closed the store. Those old pop machine and Coke signs now sell for big bucks at antique shops, but I don't know what she got for them. Mom turned the area that had been the store into a bedroom and expanded the living room.   With her family raised, Mom could now relax, but she could not retire. After working for a supermarket, she went to work at J.C. Press as a typesetter and assembler.

There were a few things along the way that make you wonder how we made it through. Owatonna, a town of about 10,000, had many corner grocery stores like ours, but now they are rare. I still have those bells that hung over the door at Matejcek Grocery and jingled every time a customer walked in or out, and whenever I see or hear them, they bring back a flood of memories.

Don Matejcek is a fleet maintenance technician for Owatonna Public Utilities. In 1963 he was a founding member of The Owatonna Diving Club, one of the Midwest's largest and most active SCUBA organizations

After a heavy snow, I shoveled the roof so that ice dams wouldn't form.

Cutting the Cord
by Bernice Lanik

If it had not been for a remarkable event on February 27, I don't know if the winter of 1937 would stand out so vividly in my mind. Because of that important and surprising event, however, I remember many things about that winter when I was twenty years old.

I was in my second year of teaching at the brick school at Pleasant Ridge about a mile and a quarter from our house, but I still lived at home. On weekends, I ran around with a large group of friends, and we had lots of fun going to barn dances, house parties, weiner roasts and scavenger hunts. One of our favorite winter pastimes was ice skating. Sometimes we drove to Winona to skate on the lake or at the East End Rink. Frequently we drove to Homer, where an area of the Mississippi River was kept clear for skating. To keep warm, we'd build a bonfire.

Not every young adult in those Depression days owned a car, so in our entire group there were only two cars available. But we made do. One time we squeezed ten people into a car--people sat on other people. Everyone, including the driver, wore skates.

A highway patrolman pulled us over, and we all thought, "Wow, what's wrong?"

The officer came over to the car and said, "Did you know that one of your headlights is out?" He looked into the car and said, "Gee--there are a lot of you in there. Where are you going?"

The driver told him we were going skating, and he made no negative reply, so we happily drove off to our destination. That was the era of the friendly cop.

We had a great many enjoyable outings that winter, and I was looking forward to an ice skating party on Saturday, February 27. Around noon, however, it began to snow, and the weather became progressively worse until we were in a real blizzard. What a disappointment! There would be no skating tonight, no good time with the crowd.

Mother cooked the evening meal and then said she was not feeling well. She went to her bedroom to lie down while my sister Lucille and I washed the dishes and finished our usual chores.

Dad went to see how Mother was feeling. Almost immediately he came out of her room in a state of agitation and concern.

"Bob, hitch the horses to the sleigh and go get Mrs. Pries. I'll call and tell her you're coming. Bernice--you go to your mother. The rest of you, go upstairs. Your mother is having a baby."

Stupid me, I hadn't even realized my mother was pregnant! Women didn't flaunt or even discuss pregnancy, and clothing styles did a lot to hide it. On top of all that, my mother never talked about anything having to do with the facts of life.

Although Mrs. Pries lived less than a mile away, she did not get to our house in time. My dad and I delivered my youngest sister Nancy that night. I don't remember all the details, but I remember my mom telling me how to cut and tie the cord. My sister Joanne remembers listening curiously and anxiously from the other room and finally hearing the cry of a newborn.

Thinking back, I thank God there were no complications, because I would have felt forever guilty if something had gone wrong--even though I had no idea what I was doing. As a farm kid, I had not even witnessed the birth of livestock; we were sheltered from that type of thing. Although I had six other younger siblings, and all but two were born at home, I had not been present for their entry into the world. Helping with Nancy's birth was my first and only turn as a midwife.

The next day the snow stopped falling, the plows cleared the road, and my father drove in to town to get a nurse. She stayed about a week to tend to Mom and the new baby. Neighbors, who were digging out after the blizzard, received news of our blessed event in a melancholy mode and told us that at the same time little Nancy was taking her first breath, our beloved elderly neighbor, who lived a mile down the road, passed out of this life. Such was the circle of life.

Because of our age difference, I felt more like a mother than a sibling to Nancy, who was only four years older than my first child. My mother and father died when Nancy was a teenager, so my husband and I helped her out and assumed some parenting responsibilities. She lived with my family when she went to college, and she was more like a cousin than an aunt to my children.

The memorable thing about that winter of 1937 was the surprise arrival of a baby sister at a time when I was caught up in the social life of a young woman and the professional life of a young teacher. At a time when I was cutting the cord in a figurative way by establishing a life apart from my immediate family, I found myself literally cutting the cord to help my mother with the birth of her last baby.

Bernice Lanik, a retired teacher, lives in Winona with her husband Charles. She enjoys doll collecting, traveling, and visiting with her four children ten grandchildren and four great-grandchildren.

Skipper
by Bernice Lanik

Growing up on a farm, my sisters, brothers and I always had a dog or two to keep us company. I especially remember Shep, a beautiful light brown and white Collie. When my little sister Joanne was a few months old and the days were warm and sunny, Mother would take a large wicker buggy outside and put Joanne in it. Shep would lie down beside the buggy and guard over my baby sister.

For fear of spoiling the child, my parents did not spare the rod. We did get spanked, and deservedly so. When Shep was around, however, he opposed and prevented corporal punishment. He would bark at our father, grab his pants leg, and pull. It was easier for Father to discontinue punishment than battle with the dog.

After my marriage, we lived on a farm with my husband's parents for about seven years. Of course, our two children, Janice and George, had a farm dog as a constant companion.

When we moved to Winona, however, I did not think we should have a dog. Since our family was growing and our living space was smaller, owning a dog did not fit into the scheme of things, but my resolve was broken by chance. Edstrom Photography had a registration for prizes. First prize was a radio, and although I didn't expect to win anything, my children insisted I register. Well, to make a long story short, I didn't win first prize. But I did win second prize-- a purebred brown Cocker Spaniel puppy. Although this was a surprise, we all fell in love with Skipper, a beautiful, friendly puppy.

Since it was December and cold, we spread papers around the house and padded a box for him to sleep in. Actually, he was very intelligent, and it didn't take long to housebreak him.

One below-zero evening, we were getting ready for bed. We looked around the house, but could not find Skipper! Had he somehow gotten outside? Up to that time he had not been out alone. Everyone bundled up and went outside to look for him because we were all very concerned. Where was he? There was no way he could survive in the cold.

We called for him and looked in every imaginable place, but still no Skipper. Finally we gave up and came back into the house. The children were crying, insisting they could not go to bed without finding Skipper. I went to hang my coat in a small closet in one of the bedrooms, and guess what I found? Yes, there he was sound asleep in the bottom of the closet. He never knew he was missing.

We lived in a house across the street from Safranek's Butcher Shop. Skipper went out to do his duty for a few minutes, and I heard scratching on the door. He was back. He walked over to me, dropped a frozen rat on the floor, looked up with a smile on his face and wagged his tail. Should I say thanks?

Sometime later, after we moved to the house we still live in behind Lake View Drive-In, he presented me with a frozen fish. Again, he was proud of his offering.

Skipper was a source of pleasure and enjoyment to our four children and the neighborhood children. When our children were older and not always available, younger neighbors would ask if they could take Skipper for a walk. He liked the attention and would often get his leash and carry it to them. However, he would only go so far and then insist on turning around to head back home. When he got older, if someone other than family wanted to take him for a walk, he did not always choose to go. He would go to a favorite spot, lie down, and look up as if to say, "No, please, not today."

He loved to ride in the car, especially if we were going out to the farm. He stood on the seat and looked out the window until he realized where we were going. If we were headed downtown, he would lie on the back seat and take a nap. If we were headed for the wide open spaces, he stayed by the window anticipating a walk in the woods exploring by himself.

The last thing Skipper chose to eat was dog food. His dish sat on a newspaper in the kitchen. If his meal was something he didn't want, he would scratch the paper from under the dish and maneuver the paper with his nose so that it covered the dish. He preferred people food.

The mailman, who carried dog biscuits, was a favorite friend of Skipper's. Skipper knew what time the mail was delivered, so he waited on the driveway for the mailman. After giving a friendly tail wagging response to his friendly greeting, Skipper would accept the dog biscuit and eat it. He would never eat our dog biscuits.

Skipper was too friendly to be a watch dog. During part of Skipper's life, the daily paper was delivered by a boy riding a bicycle. He and paper boys had always been friends. When a new paperboy started delivering papers, we could not understand why Skipper barked at him. Later we learned that he had kicked and hit our pet. Skipper never stopped barking at that boy. When a new paperboy took over the route, Skipper stopped barking and made friends with him.

Skipper sought both education and religion. When our daughter Janice was in a classroom on the second floor of Washington Kosciesko School, Mr. Sweeney, the principal, came into the classroom.

"There's a dog outside the door. Does he belong to any of you?"

Yes, it was Skipper. Janice did not know he had followed her or how he had gotten into the building. Evidently he was outside the school and either sneaked in or was let in by someone. Cocker Spaniels are gifted with a keen sense of smell, so he must have tracked her through the building to the second floor.

Our children attended St. John's Church School. Most of the boys attending the school were altar boys who assisted the priest with the mass. One day during summer vacation, our oldest son George was scheduled to serve mass. He, the priest, and another altar boy were standing in the sanctuary when through the door of the sacristy walked Skipper, as proud as could be. "Look, I found you!"   George had to stop what he was doing and take Skipper outside. Janice, who had gone to church with George, had the privilege of escorting Skipper home.

Somehow Skipper knew when we were planning a family vacation, and he also knew he would be left behind. Ours were camping vacations, and four children, two adults and camping gear left no room in the car for a dog. Shortly after we would begin to get things together, he would start spunking and sulking. He'd give us what I call glaring looks when we came near him. Grandpa Lanik usually came to dog sit. I remember one particular time when we came home after about ten days and found Grandpa and Skipper enjoying the company of one another. Skipper would have nothing to do with any of us. When Grandpa left to go home, Skipper went out the door after him and started down the street with him as if to say, "I'll show you who's my true friend."

Skipper had a jealous streak. One time my sister Joanne stopped at our house to show us a new puppy she had just gotten. Joanne put her coat on a chair in the kitchen, where we were all congregated. Of course, everyone made a big fuss over the cute little Pomeranian ball of fur. Skipper tolerated the clucking and cooing for a while, then looked at Joanne, walked over to the chair where her coat was, raised his leg and peed on her coat. He looked at Joanne again, walked to his favorite spot in front of the heat register, and stretched out.

As Skipper grew older, he was nearly blind, and he developed arthritis or rheumatism that made it difficult for him to get up and down the steps when he went outside. When he had his last walk in the woods, he had to be carried up the hill to the car. He died in the spring of 1965.

I believe he had a good fourteen years with us. He was buried by a rose bush with ceremony in our back yard. I appreciate the random luck that changed my mind and brought Skipper into our lives, but we never had another dog.

Skipper and my son Ken

Tap Dance Scam
by Myrle Solomon Erlich

When I was about 8 years old, the "Music Man" came to International Falls in the guise of Miss Lipke, the dance instructor.

Miss Lipke cajoled the grade school principal into releasing names and phone numbers of his pupils, and then she contacted parents with an offer few could resist.

Your_____is an exceptional student! I'm here to offer your child an opportunity to enhance his popularity, poise, and agility through tap dancing lessons. Every wonderful child, just like yours, should have this chance! Now, as a special introductory offer, I'm willing to charge only $3 for the entire series of five lessons! (Paid in advance, of course.)

Three dollars was a large amount of money in the Depression 30's, but parents will sacrifice for a child. My parents signed me up.

Saturday morning arrived, and we were positioned in rows across the floor of the Moose Lodge meeting room. Miss Lipke stood on the little stage in front of the class and welcomed us to our exceptional opportunity.

She waved her hands, and with a dazzling smile announced, "The first thing we are going to learn is the basic tap dance step." She demonstrated the forward-back-stamp with first her right and then her left foot. The staccato sound of her taps was exhilarating.

"Now, here we go together," she smiled. "Sweep, sweep, stamp." First our right feet and then our left. Forward-back-stamp. We practiced over and over. Finally, when we were all doing the same thing at the same time, she played the piano. I'll never forget. She played "I'm a Yankee Doodle Dandy." Gloryosky! One lesson and I was tap dancing to music.

Miss Lipke dismissed the class with a beautiful smile and a reminder, "Be sure to practice. See you all next Saturday--same time, same place!"

The next Saturday we buzzed excitedly as we waited for the Moose Lodge door to open. We tried the sweep-sweep-stamp on the sidewalk. The boys grumbled. How could tap dancing help on the football or baseball field? We waited a long time at that locked door. First the boys left. Finally we all got tired of waiting. We left and went home.

You guessed it. Our parents were victims of the "Music Man" con artist scam. Miss Lipke, like Professor Harold Hill, was just a couple of buffalo steps ahead of the law. First she took the money our parents paid her, and then she took the next train out of town.

But all was not lost. The magic of sweep-sweep-stamp remained with me. Fifty-three years later, another golden opportunity presented itself when a St. Paul community center promoted a show featuring the over-fifty crowd. Here I am again, positioned in a row of dancers across the stage. This time I have a routine consisting of time steps, pivots, Susie Q's, pinwheels and trenches. I wear a costume, wave a little American flag, and sport a top hat. Gloryosky! I'm dancing to "Yankee Doodle Dandy" all over again!"

Myrle Solomon Erlich grew up during the Depression in International Falls. She published a collection of memoirs and belongs to a senior writing group in St. Paul.

Downtown International Falls, as it looked back then.

My Piano Teacher, Miss Patricia Lynch
by Myrle Solomon Erlich

I clumped slowly up the stairs, swinging my blue and yellow music books. I was in no hurry to confront my nemesis. At the landing, I turned right, sighed deeply, and inched down a short hall. The door at the end was closed. I stopped and listened. If I heard piano music, I would wait, and if there was no sound, I would knock.

The door opened onto a room filled with clutter. Files of newspapers, magazines, sheet music and etudes decorated the floor. A narrow pathway led to a beautiful ebony grand piano. Perfectly tuned, free of dust or clutter, the piano glistened in the minimal light allowed through a smudged window. A calico cat smirked from its window seat.

My piano teacher, Miss Patricia Lynch, lived and worked in this home/studio/apartment. She was short and squat with hair trimmed into a 20's bob that framed a face half filled with steel-rim glasses that emphasized her myopic blue eyes. Miss Lynch wore a loose fitting house dress or kimono, and her bosom was always peppered with food stains.

She invariably held a cup of tea, and she frequently excused herself to refresh her cup in the kitchen. Whether she added another ingredient to compensate for my lack of talent remains a matter of speculation.

Miss Lynch took care of her elderly father, who sometimes appeared dressed in long sleeved underwear and trousers held up by suspenders. He always needed a shave, and he carried a distinctive odor which I later defined as a combination of liquor and urine.

My musical talent was expressed in properly fingered scales and eventually recognizable tunes--learned to the steady tick-tock of the metronome. Miss Lynch always gave me suggestions for improvement that began with, "Myrle, maybe if you would devote more time to practice....."

These half-hour lessons cost fifty cents. At that rate, I have calculated that "Moonlight Sonata," complete with appropriate swaying and head movements, cost my parents $52. It made for a swell recital piece, and my parents were so proud.

Class Reunions for Better or Worse
by Donna Pierce Woodward

I stood with a group of classmates at the 20th Albert Lea High School class reunion. We were commenting on how good we looked. I complimented "Koot," whom I thought looked much better than he had at the last reunion.

He patted his paunch and said, "Well, I could lose 50 pounds."
"Fifty pounds!!" I yelped. It sounded like a ton.

Then I paused, thought about it, and said, "Come to think of it, I've gained 20 pounds since we graduated."

Koot looked down from his 6'4" height and calmly said, "But, Donna, you needed it." Best reunion ever.

Years later, I attended the 45th class reunion. All through the years, I thought I had danced with Bobby during a halftime performance at the high school when we were in second grade. He had been my boyfriend from first through fourth grade, although he didn't know it.

At the reunion five years previously, we'd had a nice visit. I told him he had been my favorite dancer at that performance. He said no, he had danced with Carolyn. I didn't believe him. Carolyn was at that 45th reunion and confirmed it. She had danced with Bobby and had a photo to prove it. Besides that, he had once come to her birthday party and had given her a present!! So there!

She remembered I had danced with Moe. Moe? Moe who? She pointed him out, so I approached him, thinking I could salvage my bruised ego. In a flattering voice I told him I thought Bobby was the good dancer in second grade, but I just found out he had been my charming partner. He remembered the dancing and the basketball game, then looked at me and said, "But I don't remember you." Worst reunion ever.

Donna Woodward lived in Burnsville before retiring. She and her husband Don travel to warm climates in their 40' RV during winter and spend summers in Minnesota.

I Forgot to Vote
by Tarrie Swenstad

Odin, a prairie town located in south central Minnesota near St. James, has a population of about 105. You wouldn't think a town that size could attract national attention, but we made national news twice in twenty years.

If the name Odin sounds vaguely familiar, you may have heard it mentioned between 1979 and 1981 when Iranians held hostage Americans from the embassy in Teheran. Bruce Laingen, U.S. charge d'affaires in Iran, was one of the American diplomats taken hostage, and while they were held hostage and when they were finally released, reporters talked about how Bruce had grown up on a farm near Odin. Those of us who knew him as a kid were proud and happy to join the millions who welcomed Bruce home.

But that was not the first time our town made national news. The first time we made headlines came as the result of the outcome of the election of 1960. Everyone knows that Kennedy defeated Nixon in a hotly contested, close, and controversial Presidential bid. What many people do not know is that in the town of Odin, Duane Winters defeated incumbent Henry Swenstad for the office of mayor. You might be wondering how news like this could possibly grab national headlines.

In a town like Odin, as you might expect, the office of mayor is not a full-time job. The mayor of Odin has neither the work load nor the salary paid to the mayor of New York, Chicago or Los Angeles. He has no press secretary, no official residence, no entourage. He actually has no salary aside from a small honorarium. The mayor of Odin needs to have a day job. But still, being mayor of Odin carries responsibilities, and whoever carries out the work of mayor is elected by the usual political process. You might still be wondering how our election got national coverage.

My father-in-law, Henry Swenstad, had been mayor for several years when he was opposed by Duane Winters in the 1960 race. Henry, a carpenter, woke up the morning of election day and got so busy getting ready to drive down to Iowa with a work crew that he forgot to vote. When he returned home that night, the poles were closed and he was surprised to learn that Duane had defeated him--by one vote.

Our local news reporter, Ruth Hammer, thought this was an interesting story, so she sent it to the St. James Plaindealer and to the Mankato Free Press. Someone from Associated Press picked it up, and newspapers across the nation ran the story as a filler. Scouts for the television show "I've Got a Secret" saw the news item and invited Henry to New York to appear on the show.

At first, Henry refused. He had never been to New York, had never appeared on television, and had never flown on an airplane. He had no intention of appearing on the show. But family and friends convinced him to change his mind. My husband Donald took his dad to St. James to buy him a new suit, and we drove him to Wold- Chamberlain Airport in Minneapolis and put him on the plane for his Wednesday night show appearance. When Henry arrived in New York, someone from CBS met him at the airport, and they rolled out the red carpet and put him up at a nice hotel.

"I've Got a Secret" was a very popular show that was on the air for fifteen years. The way the show worked was that a contestant came on and whispered a secret to host Garry Moore. At the same time, the words of the secret appeared across the bottom of the screen so the viewers at home could see it. A panel of four celebrities could not see the words, so they would take turns asking the contestant questions so they could try to guess the secret. The longer it took for the panel to guess, the more money the contestant made. Top prize was a couple of hundred dollars--twice the annual mayor's salary.

The show usually featured three regular people and one celebrity with a secret. Most shows didn't have a theme, but this one did-- the importance of each person's vote.

Henry's secret that flashed across the screen when he whispered in Garry Moore's ear was, "I lost the election by one vote--and I forgot to vote." Henry stumped the panel.

Henry returned to Odin with a photo of himself with some celebrities who were on the show--Garry Moore and Helen Hayes. He was glad we had convinced him to accept the invitation to appear on the show, and we were all glad too because we enjoyed our fifteen minutes of fame almost as much as he did. The photo hangs today in the Odin Town Hall with pictures of other town events. What happened to the winner of the election? Nothing quite so exciting. He served as mayor for eight years and never enjoyed as much attention as the man who lost the election.

Tarrie Swenstad is a former sixth grade teacher at the Butterfield Odin school. She helped put together the Odin Centennial Memory book.

"I lost the election by one vote--and I forgot to vote." Garry Moore, Henry Swenstad and Helen Hayes.

It's Not What You Say; It's What You Don't Say
by Mabel Nordby

I could write a book about my fifteen years in the telephone office, but I'll share this one story. In the late 1920's, we had the telephone office in our home in Odin so that people could have night service.

One morning when I was at the switchboard, I had a long distance call from Granada, a little town south of Mankato, near Wells. Mrs. Werner Hess wanted me to get a message to Mary Van Duesen that her daughter Helen was ill. She mentioned something about a headache, but didn't say there was anything serious.

I told her I'd do my best, but since Mary didn't have a phone, it was going to be tricky. Helen was a beautiful young girl who had gone to work for Mrs. Hess because her mother wouldn't give her any money.

I watched for Helen's brother Orval to come by, as he usually did, but today he fell out of his usual habit and never came by all morning. I called different places to see if anyone was available to deliver the message, but there was no one.

Well, finally Orval came by, and I ran out to tell him. Instead of going back to tell his mom, however, he walked uptown. I had no way of knowing when he went home, and I had no right to tell him where to go or when to go there.

Some time that day, Helen died of spinal meningitis. Because of the nature of the illness, her funeral was held outdoors at Long Lake Church. I sang with the quartet, and we went together and bought flowers. A day or so after the funeral, someone rapped at my back door and here stood Mary. She said to me in a singsong way, "Mabel, do you think it does any good to sing in the choir and lay flowers on the grave when you stabbed Helen in the heart?"

I couldn't believe what I was hearing! I told her I had given Orval the message but that he had gone uptown. I think she had a guilty conscience about her daughter going out of town to get a job, and she was taking it out on me. Mary kept coming every day for a while, repeating the same thing she had said before, and I was getting pretty upset. She finally quit coming, for which I was thankful.

The manager of the telephone company in Mountain Lake called me and told me Mary had gone in there and tried to get me fired. He asked her if she had a phone, and of course she didn't.

He said, "What did you expect Mabel to do--leave the switchboard and bring you the message?" She didn't get far with him.

Orval moved to Wisconsin, and pretty soon his mother moved there too. It must have been fifteen or so years later when Mary came back to Odin for a visit. I heard a knock at my door, and when I opened it, there stood Mary. I thought, "Oh, oh. I'm going to hear her tale of woe again."

But Mary never mentioned the phone message, Helen or the funeral. We just chatted and had coffee. I think this very civil get-together was a silent apology from her. I was so thankful she came so that I could get the whole incident off my mind.

All the people in this story have died. Mabel Nordby lived in Odin for most of her life and contributed this story to Odin's Centennial Book.

True Neighbors in Odin
by Arleen Syverson Ayers

I love to think back on my childhood days in Odin many years ago. I lived with my mother, father, two sisters and two brothers, and I was the oldest child. We lived in an apartment over the P. C. Hansen Grocery and Dry Goods Store. We had a lot of steps to go up and down, but we did not mind. We kept warm in winter with a hard coal heater.

My dad worked on the railroad section and also had a job with the local elevator shoveling coal in the winter from railroad coal cars into the coal chutes going into the elevator bins. He came home with his face as black as pitch from coal dust, and it took two to three basins of water to wash it off. My mother was a seamstress who sewed dressy dresses for ladies who lived in and around Odin, and when they came for a fitting, their laughter always made it fun.

The one thing that will stick in my mind forever was the goodness and generosity of the Odin people. In the early 20's, we had an outbreak of scarlet fever. This was a very contagious disease that could cause serious after-effects, so a quarantine ordinance went into effect. If a family member contracted the disease, no other member of that family could go out in public, and nobody outside the family, except a doctor or nurse, could go inside the house. A "Do Not Enter" sign that hung outside our door to remind people the quarantine had to be obeyed for three weeks.

Of course, our family got the disease-- all except my mother. We were very sick--even my dad. My sister had a terribly sore throat, and the glands on her neck were swollen. My mother called the doctor, and he told her to follow a remedy in a medical book we had. The article described how to make an onion poultice by cooking some onions a bit and putting them into a cloth bag, and applying the bag to the sore spot on her neck. My mother did that, and lo and behold, it helped.

Scarlet Fever hit us right at Christmas time, so we could not partake of any programs or parties, which made us all sick at heart. No Christmas tree or Santa Claus to look forward to! We were nearing the last days of the quarantine one day when we heard a commotion out in the hall and a loud knock on our door.

My mother opened the door, and there stood some young women. They shouted "Merry Christmas to you!!"

We were surprised and stunned, and even more so when they gave us gifts. These caring, thoughtful ladies had gone around town soliciting money to purchase gifts for our family.

My sisters and I each received a beautiful doll, one brother got a set of Tinker Toys and a ball, and my little brother got a toy cast iron Model T Ford, which we still have in the family. It's like new, and remains a memento of a very happy Christmas. We also received candy, nuts, oranges and apples. I still remember that day and the happiness we felt when those generous and thoughtful people reached out to our family

Arlene Syverson was born and raised in Odin, and moved to St. James after her marriage. Two of her siblings still live in that area.

There Once Were Two Men from St. Clair
by Nicholas John Cords

John Cords

My earliest recollections of my grandfather are vague and intermixed with those of many other grown-ups. When I was about 4 years old, however, our family moved from downtown St. Clair to its eastern edge--about two and a-half blocks. My father, Arthur, built a new house there, and it was ready for occupancy.

My whole world seemed to change a great deal as a result of this move. The new house and location were exciting, of course, and there were new people in my life. The most important and memorable of these was my grandfather John. Our new house was located next to his farm's pasture, so I enjoyed much more contact with him than ever before. I spent a lot of time hanging around him and the farm--my mother thought too much. In time, I came to see my presence there as not only fun, but crucial. My role, in my mind, had become that of co-manager.

Grandpa at first seemed to be a large, gruff man who was always in charge of things. He was a member of a fairly large family of boys, orphaned by age 12, and raised by a neighbor and friend. I suspect that had something to do with his independent spirit. I found early on, however, that underneath that gruff exterior he was sensitive and soft-hearted. He could be stern, though. I remember once in the spring, when I was about 8, he stopped his car--a 1929 Model A Ford--downtown and chewed me out for sitting on a cold, wet cement step: "Catch Your Death!" I was embarrassed to be reprimanded in public.

Mostly, it was fun. Grandpa still did some farming and used horses, not having his own tractor. I loved horses, and occasionally he would let me ride with him and even hold the reins. I thought I was driving. Two were black work horses, but the third, Dan, was another story. Dan was brown and sleek with a white diamond in the center of his forehead. Highly spirited, he wasn't a good work horse, but Grandpa used to hitch him between the other two when doing heavy work, like plowing--arguing that once you got Dan going in the right direction, he might just pull a bit. More than a little cussing seemed also to be a necessary ingredient.

I liked Dan so much that I offered to buy him from Grandpa for a nickel I had saved--an immense sum for a young boy during Depression 30's. Grandpa was very touched, and we ultimately struck a deal-- I would own Dan, but he would care for him and use him until I was old enough to take over. I got to keep the nickel. Heck of a deal, I thought!

When younger, Grandpa owned a steam engine and a threshing machine (separator) with Jake Chase. They did custom work, following a circuit around the area. The threshing season would last from late July well into fall. Farmers had to wait their turn, so they would "stack" bundles of grain to keep the inward-turned grain heads protected and dry. Weather permitting, they sometimes worked into the winter, doing cleanup. Grandpa told of once threshing in February. Usually, however, they used the steam engine during winters to run a sawmill.

When I was hanging around, Grandpa was farming on shares with the Schwanke brothers, Aaron and Hank. He had been out of the custom business for some time. The Schwankes owned their own threshing machine, but when threshing at John Cords' they let him take over. As I got a little older, he let me handle the spout that poured grain into a box wagon. Did I feel important! As I write this, I can still hear him shout at me when I wasn't paying attention: "Nicky, dammit, don't let the wheat spill on the ground!"

Grandpa's threshing days were his glory time; he became sort of a legend concerning the management of the rig and crew. One of the old-time farmers, by the name of Ireland, liked to tell of the time Grandpa and Jake were scheduled to be at his place on a given day. As the day was actually dawning, Ireland heard a clamor on the road; it was the approaching threshing crew. Also distinguishable was the commanding voice of John Cords, urging the outfit forward with very colorful language. Grandpa's orders to Mr. Ireland were to "get your men on the damn stacks so we can begin threshing at 9 o'clock, as scheduled!"

Grandpa owned another distinction regarding his steam engine. Once, when he was crossing the LeSueur River just north of St. Clair, the bridge gave way, and the entire outfit crashed to the riverbed below. I understand that it took some doing, and no doubt much swearing, to raise the steam engine. A new bridge had to be built.

The bridge gave way and the entire outfit crashed to the riverbed below.

Grandpa died in April, 1939, when I was 9 years old and in fourth grade. He had been bothered by heart trouble for some time, but I didn't know how serious it was, and I hadn't seen nearly as much of him during wintertime as I did during summer vacation. I dreamed of him the night before he died; you can imagine how this influenced my young, impressionable and superstitious mind. The wake and services were held at the farm home prior to an afternoon burial at the Bestman Cemetery. My father had tried to arrange for services and burial at the Lutheran church and cemetery, but due to an earlier falling-out between a minister and Grandpa--that independent spirit again--that was not to be.

During the wake and amidst commotion in the small farmhouse, I experienced, for the first time in my life, the jolting pain of loss. It was gnawing; it would not go away. I have experienced it many times since, for example, at the deaths of my eldest son, parents and sister, but never more sharply than that first time. It would pass as life went on and I returned to school, but quite frankly, it doesn't take much, even now, to rekindle at least some of that emotion following Grandpa's death.

By the scheduled burial time, a ferocious spring snowstorm had arisen. Chains had to be put on the hearse and a couple of cars in order to negotiate the trip to the cemetery. Very few of the mourners attended the burial; I'm not even sure that Grandma did. It was perhaps a good thing emotionally for me that I was not allowed to go along.

I have Grandpa's favorite rocking chair--the chair in which he spent most of his nonworking waking hours. It sat in the kitchen where most of our chats occurred. It was there where my purchase of Dan transpired. My wife, Maggie, thoughtfully stripped the chair of its many coats of paint (Grandpa was a great painter), varnished it and had it re-caned. I spend a lot of time sitting in it reading, and rarely do so without fondly remembering Grandpa John Cords.

Frank Cords

Frank wasn't really my uncle--he was my great-uncle, the youngest brother of my grandfather, John. Like John, Frank was orphaned at a very early age and was raised by an aunt. John, some eight years older, looked after Frank, and later Frank lived for a time with John and his wife Clara. The result of this was the development of a very close bond between these two brothers, a bond that lasted until John's death in 1939. Frank was a large man for the times, standing over six feet tall and weighing approximately 190 pounds. He was outgoing, confident, and extremely adventurous. As you might imagine, he led a very interesting life.

At age 17 he enlisted in the U.S. Army to serve in the Spanish-American War. He liked to tell of the time when his company was stationed at Chattanooga, Tennessee. One day when the order was given to fall out (assemble), only he and one other man appeared--the result of flu and dysentery. Frank said that he didn't feel too sharp either, but he didn't want to miss any possible excitement. I believe the war was over before he got to Cuba, although he did spend about seven weeks there.

After the war he finished high school, traveled, wrestled, worked as a fireman on the railroad, a ranch hand, a farmer, an insurance and car salesman, and construction worker. In 1909 he married Clarissa Nelson, and they had two children-- Willard and Verna.

Regarding his on-again-off-again wrestling career, Frank related this story: He was following the county fair and carnival circuit somewhere in Michigan because this was where many wrestling opportunities existed. There was one particularly good wrestler who was beating all challengers.

Rather than challenge him immediately and possibly lose, Frank followed the man on the circuit for awhile and bet on him to win--a profitable enterprise. All the while, Frank was scouting the man and getting to know his strengths and weaknesses. Then came the challenge. Frank beat him and walked away with the prize money. By this time, the two men were acquainted because the other man noticed Frank consistently in the crowds. Evidently Frank's cleverness was recognized, if not totally appreciated.

In 1926, Frank ran for the office of Blue Earth County Sheriff. I don't know the specifics concerning the campaign, except that his wife Clarissa told me about how hard the family worked on it. Even their young son Willard delivered handbills and encouraged all to vote for his dad--"the best dad in the world." Frank won, and served in that capacity for twenty years.

I got to know Frank personally during this period, which was fun and exciting. Because of the bond between Frank and my grandfather John, I'm sure it's safe to say that we saw more of him in St. Clair than we otherwise would have.

He made frequent visits to John at the farm, confiding in him and I think showing off a bit for his older brother, whom he had always admired. Frank got involved in one of the abortive attempts to capture John Dillinger in Minnesota. A result of this was that one of Dillinger's cars, a Hudson, showed up in Mankato. Frank drove the car to St. Clair and up the hill to the farm to show John--horn blaring all the way.

On his visits to St. Clair, he invariably stopped at Dad's barbershop, and sometimes at our house. Once in awhile he would stop to talk to me on the street--did I feel important! Frank represented my encounter with celebrity. He was my hero, and he was my uncle--well, at least, my dad's uncle.

Being a sheriff then was sort of a frontier job. Sheriffs today tend to function in more of an administrative capacity, with multiple deputies to do field (grunt) work.

Frank never had more than one or two deputies, one of whom operated the switchboard, so Frank did all the grunt work. If the services of the sheriff were needed, it was invariably Frank who showed up. His life was exciting and sometimes dangerous.

If there was, say, a dangerous fight situation at a barn dance out in the county somewhere, Frank many times showed up alone. He was armed, of course, but firing a gun was a last resort. I asked him once how he handled a situation such as that, and he told me that he quickly tried to focus on the chief troublemaker, isolate him, talk to him and, failing that, take him on!

On one occasion, a dangerous at-large criminal who had made threats about what he physically was going to do to Frank if he ever had the chance, was arrested by police and brought to Frank at the jail. Frank gave him his chance. I don't know the details, but it seems that he made a move, whereupon Frank hit him on the jaw, breaking it in three places.

It wasn't all roughhouse, however. These were the Depression years, and many inmates at the jail received counsel, care, and help finding a job from Frank and his wife. I remember Frank saying to one departing inmate, "Don't let me see you here again! I'll give you all the help I can, but don't ever let me see you here again!"

Probably my happiest memories of Frank Cords involve the times when I stayed with him at the jail and accompanied him on his rounds. He seemed to know everyone and have something to say to each, usually in the form of advice, sometimes developing into a lecture or sermon.

Frank was a fast, some might say reckless driver. The car I particularly remember was a gray 1939 Buick coach, with his stop sign on the fender. He seemed to drive it at top speed all the time. I checked the speedometer as we drove down the alley behind the jail once, and it read 45 m.p.h.!

I accompanied him when he escorted a prisoner to the St. Cloud Reformatory. As we entered the outskirts of Mankato on the way home, I thought he was stopping for some reason and reached for the door handle. He informed me that we were doing 50 m.p.h.--after 85-90 on the highway.

The most exciting event, however, occurred one day about noon in downtown Mankato on the main drag--Front Street. Frank asked me if I wanted to have some fun; I replied in the affirmative. He then ran the entire length of Mankato at 50 m.p.h., with the siren going full blast, and he laughed as cars scurried to get out of the way of this apparent emergency.

Attending the Blue Earth County Fair at Garden City was another spectacular event. As sheriff of the county, Frank had to be there every day, sometimes more than once. This was like heaven on earth for me. He would deposit me at the fair in the morning and pick me up at night, making sure, of course, that I was supplied with enough money. It was a blast! It was so wonderful that not everyone believed I could be so lucky.

One summer there was a wrestler there who took on all comers. I was fascinated and gullible so I frequented the tent quite a bit. During one match, the tent raised behind me and an acquaintance, Joe Stegemeir, entered--without paying, of course. He had been seen slipping in, so the manager and the wrestler accosted him. Since he was talking to me, they assumed that I was Joe's accomplice. I had thrown my ticket away, so all arguments that I was with the sheriff didn't cut much ice.

"With the sheriff, yeah, right!"

The manager told Joe and me to leave and never darken the tent flap again--no problem for me. Later that day, Frank and I walked past the wrestling tent where the two men were standing out front. They saw us together, and I thought raised their eyebrows a bit, but I'm sorry to say, they did not rush to apologize to me.

Frank lost his re-election bid in 1946 to one of his deputies, a younger man and veteran of World War II. He argued that Frank was too old to effectively continue as sheriff. He won and died of a heart attack before completing his first term.

We continued to see a lot of Frank and Clarissa after Frank's retirement. He served on the Mankato City Council for a time, and continued to be an interesting and exciting character. Frank died in 1975 at age 95. I'm sorry I didn't pump him for more personal information; he surely would have been willing. He was a great storyteller. I last saw him about six months before he died, and he didn't recognize me until just before I left. That's not the Frank Cords I choose to remember

Nick Cords taught history and humanities at Albert Lea High School for six years before moving to Lakewood Community College, (now Century College) where he taught American history for twenty-six years. Now retired, he enjoys reading, writing, and playing the trombone.

One of the High Points
by Wallace Kennedy

Of the forty-one years I worked in public education, the thirteen years I spent in high school classrooms were the best. But the pay, with a family to support, made going from the classroom to supervisory jobs seem more practical. In my early years of teaching, before school breaks were spent in graduate school to make me a candidate for a supervisory job, I always had to find a summer job.

Albert Lea School District's chief of maintenance was kind enough to use teachers to supplement his custodial staff. Teachers were assigned those jobs custodian union contracts had negotiated away--painting, varnishing, and high-level carpentry that probably should have been put up for bid to local contractors. But teacher heads-of-households needed to support their families, so we took the jobs.

For several summers I was a painter/varnisher as part of a three-man team with choral music teacher, Bob Myers, and Lou Olson, a coach and social studies teacher. Bob and Lou were veteran summer supplementary custodial staff, so they brought me up to journeyman competence with masterful guidance. They were fun to work with-- great storytellers, both veterans of World War II, and both genuinely good men.

One summer our team was given the task of painting all the flag poles in front of the elementary and secondary schools and all the exposed roof metal on the school buildings--the ridge trims of pitched roofs, the variously shaped roof vents, and the oversized eve troughs found on some buildings. Flag poles required setting up scaffolding and then a ladder to let a painter reach all the way to the top.

Roof work was usually accessed through an attic trap door. No one on our team was acrophobic; in fact, we all enjoyed painting at high points outdoors where fresh air ventilation from paint and varnish fumes made work somewhat more pleasant. We were a team, making sure each member was careful and safe from accident as we worked.

Sometimes we got so engrossed in storytelling we forgot to be cautious. One morning, such was the case when working on the Central

Junior High building's slate roof. We had finished painting the ridge trim, but the various vents along the steeply slanted roof still needed paint. I scooted down to paint one such vent near the edge of the roof that stood three floors above the asphalt covered inner courtyard below.

Working around the vent, with my bucket of paint tied to my belt, I somehow tipped the paint bucket to spill part of its contents on the slate roof. We had with us a bucket of oleum spirits and a bag full of cotton rags for just such emergency, so I climbed back up to the roof ridge to get what I needed to clean up the spill. Bob said, "You better tie a rope around your waist before going down to clean that up. Slate can be awful slippery with oleum spirits."

So I ran a half inch nylon rope around my waist, tied it in a secure square knot, and left the running end of the rope with Bob to tie to one of the vent pipes close to the roof ridge. Bob was in the midst of a story about when he returned from World War II overseas duty, and that must have been why he forgot to tie the rope I depended on to the vent pipe.

I duck-walked back down to the paint spill and began cleaning up the mess, being sure not to step where the oleum spirits had been used to clean off the slate. When I finished the cleanup, I stood up and grasping the rope to help my ascent to the ridge, found the rope was sliding down the roof towards me. No problem, I was young and in good shape, and I walked up the roof pitch to its peak carrying the rope in one hand and my bucket of oleum spirits and cleanup rag in the other hand.

Bob was just finishing his story, so I waited before handing him the running end of the rope. When he saw what he'd done--neglected to secure the rope to prevent my dropping off the edge of the roof, he sat down on the roof peak, pale in the face. His apology was brief and convincing. My laugh spread to Bob and Lou, and we all three laughed loud and hearty. We now had another story to tell when we met at lunch with our fellow teachers who were also supplemental custodians.

Wally Kennedy taught English, humanities and theatre at Albert Lea High School for ten of his years in public education. Later, he created the Urban Arts Program for the Minneapolis Public Schools and helped establish the Minnesota Arts High School.

All Hail the Power
by Wallace Kennedy

My first teaching job began in January, 1953, replacing the pregnant teacher of English 9, 10, 11, and 12, at Delavan High School, just north of Blue Earth. I was also assigned to direct speech activities and the senior class play. For this I was paid $1500 for the half year of work, less withholding taxes, social security and teacher retirement.

When the school year ended, before moving to Forest Lake for my next job, I needed summer employment to support a nine month old child and pregnant wife. Joyce's dad was Superintendent of Schools in Henderson, and he was sure he could get me work at the Green Giant packing plant in LeSeuer. So we moved our meager belongings to Henderson, rented an apartment above the hardware store on main street, and I went for an interview with Green Giant's personnel manager.

As soon as he learned my boyhood had included farm work in North Dakota, the personnel manager decided I was not suited for canning factory work and hired me instead to be a pea viner foreman. Pea viners at that time were installations of two stationary threshing machines, located at a site where farm trucks hauled the cut vines from growers' fields and dumped them alongside the twelve foot long steel troughs that fed the machines.

Two viner foremen were stationed at each viner site. A tractor driver with a front shovel was there to level off the stack of threshed vines, and a team of eight men with pitchforks fed the peas into the thresher. That was the team supervised by the viner foremen.

Viner foremen were expected to get the peas threshed and to market within an hour after they were dumped alongside the feeder troughs. That meant keeping the men with pitchforks constant in a steady feed that would not choke the thresher but keep the peas falling into the boxes unbruised and whole. It also meant carrying the forty-pound boxes of peas to the shade of the viner shelter, stacking the boxes eight high, and loading them onto the trucks that carried them to the factory so they could be canned within two hours after they were field cut.

Viner foremen were paid $1.07 an hour plus a cumulative bonus of a few cents per hour if the peas reached the factory on time. Of course everything had to run in synchrony to make bonus.

In daylight there was no worry the men would slack off feeding the peas into the thresher. The glare of the metal on the twelve foot feeders begged to stay covered with vines. After sundown, the cooler air kept the pitchforkers working. That summer, the pitchforkers were Bahamians, migrant workers brought to work in the U.S. to help out the British economy back in the islands. The men who drove the stack tractor needed no supervision. The continuous arrival of empty vines kept the stack tractor drivers busy, pushing vines evenly across the stack so they would dry without mold and become good forage for feeding livestock.

There was really only one question the viner foremen had to settle. Should we shut down the threshers to grease all the moving parts every three hours, or keep them running while we grease them? The company rule was to shut the threshers down rather than risk injury or death by getting caught in the machinery. But the prudent answer was grease 'em while they're running and make the bonus. Meeting the prudent task was somewhat touchy, because at peak harvest time, viner foremen sometimes stayed on duty for as many as seventy-two hours, catching ten or fifteen minute naps at the stool in the phone booth before taking a twelve hour break.

-2-

In the humid, hot weather of the Minnesota River Valley, the apartment I shared with Joyce and Ellen was not an easy place to find sleep after grueling hours of work. It was like an oven under the roof of the two-story commercial building because there was no cross ventilation to give us a breeze. But it was a haven to come home to a beautiful wife and precious baby daughter, if only for the twelve hours off--eleven hours at home, subtracting travel time to the viner station and back.

What gives that summer with the Green Giant pea harvest a lasting memory is that the Bahamian migrant workers who pitched peas were, for me, a new experience. They were not only constantly dependable workers. They were men of courtesy, education, and thoughtful banter uncommon to field workers. Usually as they pitched peas into the viner, they sang hymns or Caribbean songs, but if they weren't singing, they often quoted verse from the King James Bible, making argumentative points about how life should be lived. During lunch breaks, they shared their life experience and culture with the rest of us.

During one lunch break, experience sharing was attached to a short history lesson. The "teacher" was a well-spoken, tall fellow named Edward. The company sent lunch out to the viners by way of a truck that hauled the peas. Lunch for the U.S. workers was cold meat sandwiches, coleslaw or potato salad, and processed pudding or cookies with a thermos of coffee or cans of soda pop. To the company's honor, lunch for the migrant workers was from their own cultural diet-- hot beans and rice, tortillas or cornbread with shredded meat or chunks of chicken, and sauces that looked far more appetizing than the cold food provided the rest of us.

The day of the history lesson, I observed that the food they were given was more nourishing than the food sent out for us. Edward, in excellent, Caribbean-flavored English, responded. "Ah, yes sir. You surely know from your history books that we black people were brought to your country and to our islands for slave labor. What you may not know is that our people were often starving at that time in Africa, because of drought, or other God-sent miseries of weather. So the Dutch man, the English man, or the rich men of your land who had slave ships, lured our people to slave captivity with the offer of beans and rice. And today, the Green Giant believes he can lure us to work for him with beans and rice, too."

One Sunday, the stack tractor broke down, and my call to the company shop gave me the message that mechanics don't work on Sundays, so there was no possible repair to the tractor. I protested that the vines were being belched out of the viners at a rate that was turning the vine stack into a small mountain range that could never be flattened out evenly if it were unattended. So the personnel office promised a team of pea pitchers to manage the stack by hand.

Within the hour, a pickup with eight Bahamians in the open back pulled up. One of the men who jumped down was Edward. He shaded his eyes with his hand as he looked at the vine stack's uneven terrain, and seeing the work that faced him and his fellows said, "All hail the power of Jesus' name, let angels prostrate fall." His epithet still stands as the most sophisticated, civil, and powerful swear word I ever heard.

The Gopher Magnate
by David J. Chrz

For kids growing up in the 50's, money didn't grow on trees. I don't suppose it did for their parents, either, but parents were reluctant to share any resources they may have had with their 12-year-olds on a cash basis. This left few avenues of capital generation for an enterprising youth such as myself.

Oh, there was an allowance all right, but parents expected you to actually do some kind of chores to earn that. Besides the ubiquitous pop-bottle redemptions, there were always sidewalks to shovel in winter, and lawns to mow in summer. If you had particularly long-suffering neighbors, you might even get to mow and shovel for the same people, but that never seemed to happen too often. Mowing had its drawbacks, too. The mowing itself wasn't so bad, but weed-eaters in those days looked suspiciously like scissors, and required you to crawl on your hands and knees around house, garage, flower beds and trees, furiously snipping away.

I really kind of enjoyed shoveling snow, except that some of my best customers lived on a stretch where the sidewalk was made of bricks, instead of concrete. The corners of those bricks were extremely hard on a shovel, as well as the shoveler's temper. What I needed was a way up and out of both poverty and work.

It's not that I was particularly avaricious, mind you, but I required some semblance of the good life. There were always bicycle accessories or repairs to buy, root beers at the A&W, and fishing lures (the gaudier the better), plus everybody needed some money to just waste.

Then one spring I hit on a plan: trapping gophers. The Minnesota state mascot is a little chipmunk-looking varmint called a gopher. He is basically harmless, and except for the old "catch a gopher on your rod-and-reel" trick, we never bothered them much. There may be a handful of readers out there, not from Minnesota, who have never heard of that trick, so I'll explain. You ride your bike about six miles out of town to the golf course, carrying your fishing rod across the handlebars.

Once there, you find a gopher hole. In between golfers, you make a slip knot in your fishing line, put a loop around the gopher hole, then let out enough line to get to a hiding place. Gophers are fairly curious, and often respond to a particular whistle, so you watch the hole, and whistle that call. If a gopher sticks his head out to look, you set the rod, thereby simultaneously snaring the gopher around his neck and snatching him out of the hole. As you reel him in, things often get pretty sporty, and you should expect to draw a crowd of golfing onlookers.

The most exciting part is the release; for most beginners I recommend cutting the line and running. That's about it; nothing could be simpler. These were called striped gophers, and as I've said, we didn't bother them much.

The gophers worth money were called pocket gophers. They are much larger than striped gophers, and live entirely underground. They look like really big moles, and make serious pests of themselves, as they harvest plant roots for food, killing large sections of lawns and crops-- so much so that individuals often paid to have them removed. Not only individuals, but also townships in those days offered a bounty on pocket gophers, and that's where I came in.

Pocket gophers can be fairly difficult to trap, as they rarely come above ground, but I eventually hit upon a successful method. It would have been easier, of course, to poison them, but most folks didn't want to spread poison around under their lawns or fields, and rightfully so, plus you had to recover the deceased gopher to collect the bounty.

I spent two memorable summers in pursuit of the wily pocket gopher--sometimes even living for days at a time with the farm family for whom I was trapping. It boggles the imagination to calculate those folks' cost per gopher removed when you factor in room, and especially board.

When I was finished and ready to leave, they would pay me, usually twenty-five cents per head. My next step would be to collect the bounty from the township in which I had caught the gophers, and I usually preferred to wait for that until just before back-to-school, when I could draw one huge lump sum.

A note here about township bounties: Of course, they required proof of performance. It was my great good fortune that Lansing Township required the front feet, while nearby Oakland Township paid on the tails, soooo........

In a good summer I might catch as many as two hundred gophers, and with the monies paid by individuals as well as the twenty-five cent and forty-cent township bounties-- well, you can do the math. Hunting gophers was Easy Street. Among other things, I went with my dad and proudly bought my first wristwatch with gopher money.

Even now, I'll occasionally hear someone use the phrase, "salting something away," and I can't help but smile, thinking of those days, when my entire net worth was out in the garage, packed in mayonnaise jars full of salt, awaiting that final bicycle ride that would turn a summer's enjoyment into spending money.

David Chrz grew up in Austin and graduated from Pacelli High School in 1965. He has lived in the Abilene, Texas area since his discharge from the US Air Force in 1975.

Wanderlust
by David J. Chrz

The scene was St. Augustine middle school, 1959, Austin, Minnesota. It was sixth grade English class, and Sister Somebody was holding a gun to our heads, trying to make us absorb poetry.

The gun was metaphorical, but it was an automatic Parental Permission to Administer Corporal Punishment caliber. It was spring, and the occasional low-flying insect dropped to the floor, stunned flightless by the overpowering stench of ennui in the air. Then it happened.

Somewhere in the first stanza of a poem by Joyce Kilmer I saw for the first time that word: "wanderlust." It leapt off the page onto my psyche, and stomped my soul into submission with little hobnail boots. Wander- lust. As a 12-year-old with a bicycle, I knew a thing or two about wandering, and I had an impersonal sense of the definition of lust (I tried on a daily basis to get more personal with it, though.) Wanderlust. That's what I had, and I had it bad. It wasn't the first time it had happened to me, either.......

Everyone gets the urge to get up and go from time to time, but once in a great while the urge becomes overpowering. The first time that urge overpowered me, I was only 5 years old, and no match for something so intense. I can only recall this episode in the overview, so my mom fleshed in the details for me.

It seems I was really put out with the whole world, or at least all of it within my ken. My sister had recently turned 2 years old, and she was probably the root cause of my disaffection with everything. I had a pretty cushy deal until she showed up. I was mad at her, mad at my parents for ordering her, mad at my grandparents for paying attention to her, mad about school starting in a couple of months, and mad at pretty much anything else that occurred to me.

Finally, enough was too much, so one afternoon I announced to Mom that I was running away. For a relative rookie, Mom was cool, sagely telling me she wished I wouldn't leave, but if I had to go, she would understand. However, if I left, I couldn't come back. Mom says this gave me pause to consider.   I thought about it for a minute or two, and then (showing early indications of a mulish nature that graces me to this day) told her through clenched teeth that I was leaving anyway.

My mother, to this day, thinks that threats uttered through clenched baby teeth are not to be taken seriously. Anyway, I had her make me a couple of sandwiches and wrap them up in a dish towel, while I had a long and heart-wrenching good-bye with my three invisible friends, Zebra, Ranger-Tanger, and Windy Lane. I slung the sandwich dish towel over my shoulder in approved apprentice hobo fashion, and put on my Davy Crockett cap.......

It would be a serious injustice not to include a word about that cap. This was a time when Fess Parker and Walt Disney ruled not only Sunday nights on TV, but great segments of my life and all my friends' lives. No matter what the item, if it didn't say "Davy Crockett," we didn't want it. The first and most obligatory article was, of course, the coonskin cap.

Whether for financial reasons, or, more likely, to avoid wasting suitable materials we already had on hand, my Mother decided to make my Davy Crockett cap. She had an old imitation fur coat whose condition had long since dictated that it no longer be worn in public, so she traced the top of my head and cut a matching oval for the first piece. She then cut about a three- inch strip out of the coat and sewed an edge of that all the way around the oval. This left only the tail, which she cut out of the coat and sewed on the back of the hat.   While my friends all had fluffy coon tail models, I had a more aerodynamic beaver tail type model which was a little threadbare, but my pride and joy.

Back to running away: Once properly attired and having said good-bye to my three imaginary friends-- the only people who cared anything about me-- I went out the front door and turned left upon reaching the front sidewalk. My mom, even though she didn't care about me, watched my progress unseen from the front steps. Once I reached the corner, I faced the first dilemma to be expected if you run away when you are 5. I wasn't allowed to cross the street by myself.

Running away and never seeing anyone again was one thing, but disobedience to this most iron-clad of rules was a horse of another color. I had little choice but to turn left again. Although I wasn't the brightest kid on the block, after left turns at the next two corners, it occurred to me that the best I could expect would probably be to live in the fort (shallow, hand-dug depression) we had built in my grandparents' field, and this just didn't have the ring of authority I was looking for because it was right next door to our house.

I made a temporary camp at the fort, ate my sandwiches, and just generally sulked around for a while. Then, being careful to arrive before my dad got home from work, I made my way back to our house. Upon arriving, I told my mom that I had made a scouting trip, and was REALLY running away tomorrow. She let me back in, despite her strict no-return policy, and actually seemed sort of glad to see me.

Years later it was spring, sixth grade, and once again, to paraphrase the poet, "Wanderlust had seized upon my feet." Standing in the hot lunch line in the cafeteria that day, I commiserated with my best friend. We discovered, to our amazement, that we had parents with equally oppressive policies regarding chores, cleanliness of sleeping quarters, cleanliness of our persons, manners, and no telling how many other trivial things. There was only one solution for our predicament--running away.

This time I was older and a lot smarter. Spur-of-the-moment flight wouldn't do. What we needed was a comprehensive plan, so we set out in that direction. The first things we needed were aliases. Once our parents realized we were gone, they would probably have the authorities look for us. Today, this alone makes me wonder if we had really thought this all the way through.

Since we planned to become mountain men, our aliases had to be suitable for that occupation. Having just watched a Clint Walker episode of "Cheyenne Bodey" the night before, my alias came to me readily-- Joe Bodus. While really cool, it wasn't as mountain man specific as I might have liked, so it took all the rest of lunch hour to come up with the second name, but it was worth the wait--Antler Carbouja.

"Joe Bodus and Antler Carbouja-Mountain Men" That had a look suitable for framing, and that's sort of how I pictured it-- carved into a wooden shingle, swinging back and forth in the wind above a board sidewalk somewhere in the mountains.

The next thing we needed was a plan to make a living in the mountains. We weren't stupid; we knew the mountain men had pretty well come and gone, but on the other hand, their scarcity left the field mostly open for a couple of rookies.

Whatever we ended up doing to support ourselves, it should be authentic, so we decided on trapping. I had some experience trapping gophers and muskrats, and even one badger who had been running my gopher trap line before I got to it, so trapping should be no problem. What proved problematic were the traps themselves.

Trapping bears, elk, mule deer, and other mountain-type stuff required traps of a size not generally available in southern Minnesota and too heavy to carry on our bikes if they had been available. Our only option was to wait until we reached the mountains, and then get together our grubstake. (What a great word; we had heard it on TV, and used it every chance we got while preparing our plan.)

After school the next Friday, we loaded up a few clothes and all the food we could pilfer from our respective kitchens, and set out for the mountains on our bikes. We had, of course, also taken all the allowance money we had managed to save during our lifetimes, but that amount was pitiful. This impoverished condition was not the result of our spending habits, but rather of our parents' penurious ways, which was one of the main reasons for running away in the first place.

The road to the mountains ran conveniently past one of our favorite places just outside the city limits, so we decided to stop and rest. We already had a ring of firestones there from squirrel hunting and fishing, so this spot along the Red Cedar River was a natural for this first of what would undoubtedly be many rest stops.

Not wanting to stop there without a fire for old times' sake, we built one. Once you have a really nice fire going, it is a shame not to cook something, as any mountain man will tell you. Basically, we ate all our food at this spot. This called for a re- evaluation of our plan; it was now apparent that the carrying capacity of our bikes was insufficient to make it out of Mower County, let alone all the way to the mountains.

Given our sorry financial situation, it was obvious that we would have to work at odd jobs along the way to buy food. The problem with this was that doing a bunch of odd jobs didn't square with our vision of being mountain men. Work was one of the main things we were running away from. Besides, why do a lot of work for strangers when you can work for your parents, and you already know what you're getting into? It was still early enough in the day to beat our parents home, so that's what we did.

We had eaten all our provisions in less than two hours, and the fact that this would probably not be an isolated occurrence dissuaded any further attempts at running away. Consequently, I've spent all my adult life rooted more or less happily in one relatively small area. Still, once in a while when the moon is blue and the wind just right, I swear I can smell Alaska, and I've upgraded my transportation from a bicycle to a pickup.......

Entertainment in Austin
by David J. Chrz

I am and have always been a true devotee of play, and just generally having fun. (My employer would attest to this, I believe.) Although I'm not sure my grandkids would recognize it as such, we had a ton o' fun as kids growing up in Austin in the 50's and early 60's. The following paragraphs are not written to inform or educate, but I intend to have a really good time remembering this stuff.

My earliest memories of play involve the neighborhood kids. We probably bore a startling resemblance to The Little Rascals. There were various dogs -- mostly mutts-- and in the few photos I have, the dogs look better than the kids.

There were forts to be dug and dirt clods to be thrown--the clods replaced by snowballs in winter. The Red Cedar River comprised the rear property lines of the houses right across the street, so we had a really handy twofer when it came to getting in Dutch; not only was I forbidden to go down to the river, but I was also forbidden to cross the street to get there. This convenient arrangement saved a lot of time, trouble, and suspense as both parents and kids pretty well knew in advance when and why the next spanking was due.

By the time we were 6 or 7, Davy Crockett and Lone Ranger paraphernalia had supplanted free style play. Cap pistols (occasionally even loaded with real caps), rifles, and coonskin caps were the uniform of the day-- every day. In a rare total lapse of good judgement, my parents bought me a Lone Ranger tent. If I don't make it into heaven, it will be at least partly their fault for making that purchase.

By the time I was about 8, my folks decided to build a new house so we moved into a rented house while construction was underway. All the kids had bikes by that age, and were extremely proficient in their use.

This changed EVERYthing. Wheeled transportation brought all the coolest entertainment into range, and first on any 8-year-old's list of cool entertainment is the City Dump.

In what could only be described as a pack, we would feverishly pedal to the dump in hopes of beating the "ragpickers" to the best junk. The ingenuity used to haul home on a bike some of the more unwieldy treasures we found defies description. Not only did this Monroe Street house boast easy access to the landfill (if you had a bike), but it also had a park with a hockey rink, and a railroad track at the end of the block.

This perfect setup allowed us to pick up broken hockey sticks at the rink and sharpen the ends to a wicked point. In the summer we would walk the tracks trying to spear the occasional rabbit or pheasant flushed along the right-of-way. A scarcity of rabbits or pheasants usually led to civil unrest, and I'm still not sure why none of us was ever speared through and through.

Sugar beets were hauled down those tracks in gently rocking open cars, so there was never a shortage of them to gnaw on as we crept along, on the alert for game and each other. Fall was a great season too, as a neighbor across the street had a small field in which he raised popcorn. I don't know about all varieties of popcorn, but his variety produced an ear of perfect throwing-size and weight, and hard as any rock.

Formal contests required a Snow Coaster (this was a round aluminum sledding dish with canvas handles on both sides). You put your arm through one handle and grasped the other, making a dandy shield that gave off a really satisfying BONG! when you deflected a shot; your head gave off a somewhat meatier BONG! when you failed to deflect a shot. Informal contests required concealment sufficient for ambush. I believe the term "pop-knot" came from these Monroe Street skirmishes.

When construction ended, a new house meant a new neighborhood and new friends. This house was on Water Street and located appropriately near East Side Lake. The hours spent fishing in those mostly sterile waters, both summer and winter, reached an embarrassingly large number.

We also were getting pretty heavily into roller-skating at about this time. Our skates were the old-time clamp-on-your-shoes skates, so we built a plywood jump. I'm certain our mothers shuddered as we worked, but what could they do?

Once the jump was finished, we tied a tow rope behind a bicycle seat. The rider pedaled furiously, the skater hung on to the rope, and at the last second the skater swerved out toward the jump in approved water-ski fashion. I clearly remember one broken arm and a broken tailbone, but I'm sure there were other casualties I've forgotten (mercifully).

This was all happening in the late 50's, and if you can recall the cars of that era, you'll understand. My next-door neighbor and I would ride over to the highway and sit on the front steps of the Lutheran church. For hours, as cars approached, we would compete to see which of us could correctly identify the make and model of a distant vehicle just by looking at its front end. Try that NOW!

Another favorite pastime was looking for agates. As the north shore of Lake Superior was a little distant for a bicyclist, we had to use the resource at hand, and that was the Ready-Mix plant. There was one particular aggregate bin that contained the occasional agate. If you could climb around on that pile long enough before the yard boss saw you and ran you off, there were treasures to be found. I still have my agate collection from those days. The easiest way to identify an agate is to moisten it and hold it up toward the sun to see if it is translucent and has stripes.

"Where are you kids going?"

"To the Ready Mix to lick rocks."

"Be back in plenty of time for supper."

Starting about this time and continuing for several years was a truly favorite pastime--swimming. Family outings were usually to the river at Lansing or the gravel pit at Owatonna, and occasionally to Lake Pepin or Roberds Lake. However, the swimming I remember best was at the Austin municipal pool. A mob of us would ride bikes clear across town to the pool. Once there, we would swim for two hours-- no admission charge in what was known as "free period." The pool was then cleared, admission charged (15 cents), and we had two hours of "pay period." We weren't often flush enough to afford "pay period," but when we could, it was great because we didn't have to contend with the "free period" riffraff -- who were friends at all times other than "pay period".

There was a snack bar at the pool, and my favorite treats when I could afford them were Sugar Babies, or a Slo-Poke caramel sucker, and a cream soda. In retrospect, a cheaper, quicker alternative snack would have been to snort a cup of sugar, but we hadn't thought of that yet.

I do not want to fail to mention winter activities. There was the usual sledding at Skinner and Whittier hills, ice fishing, cottontail hunting, and of course, skating. Usually we skated on a neighborhood rink provided by some spectacularly patient parents. Not only did they have to build and maintain the rink, but also had to put up with a herd of occasionally unruly, always loud and exuberant kids.

One of those generous parents I still remember. He was completely bald, and honestly fancied himself a serious speed skater. Every kid in the neighborhood called him "Bullet" year 'round, and I never decided if it was because of his skating or his hairdo. Once I hit the fifth grade, my favorite skating was at the municipal rinks, especially at one called "The Lagoon."

We enjoyed the usual warming house with kerosene heater, music piped out over the ice, and lights at night. However, the main attraction was the girls. Skating at night under the lights to music with your arm around a girl's waist and holding her other hand was, I thought, too hot for words. To this day, I still feel romantic when I smell a kerosene heater.

Summer evenings often found us playing the usual group games: kick the can, and Annie-I-Over among them. Who in the world dreamed up, "Annie-I-Over......... Pigtail!" And what does it mean?

The closest thing to vandalism we ever engaged in consisted of standing around a city street light for hours, throwing a rubber ball at the light. The ball wouldn't break the glass cover, but if hit just right, the cover would unlatch and hang down from the hinge side. Nothing was better than getting to watch the guy in the city cherry-picker have to re-latch the cover in a day or so. He gave us dirty looks while we pretended to be nonchalant and completely innocent.

Along about this time, I got really interested in tennis. This proved to be an excellent activity for me as I later got to play on both high school and college teams. There were not a lot of courts in Austin, and the ones I used almost exclusively were at the sports complex known simply as

"The Athletic Field." Although I spent hundreds of hours at those courts, some of my fondest memories are not of tennis.

Next door to the Athletic Field someone put in a trampoline center when that craze got underway. Music played constantly, and I KNOW I heard "Muleskinner Blues" by the Fendermen a thousand times......"Bring the buck-buck-bucket round." Besides the ubiquitous Fendermen, the drum and bugle corps known as the Lancers used the Athletic Field for marching and musical practice, and over the years I learned every note of every song they played, and I frequently marched in time to pick up stray tennis balls.

In Austin, the last momentous event before a boy got his driving Learner's Permit was getting a Shaw Gym card. The facility had been donated years earlier, and was then operated by the City Parks Department. Shaw Gym consisted of several basketball and volleyball courts, ping-pong tables, handball courts, and a boxing/wrestling ring.

The main draw, however, was the presence of about a dozen beautiful old Brunswick pool tables. If I remember correctly, once you reached seventh grade, you were eligible for your Shaw Gym card. If you were caught swearing or skipped a ball off a pool table, the supervisor punched your card. Five punches, and you were out for two weeks--the seventh grade Austin equivalent of banishment to Siberia.

There were always more prospective pool players than tables or cues, even though four players to a table was requisite, so every forty-five minutes a supervisor blew a whistle, and there would ensue a mad scramble to stab cues into a fiber barrel at the corner of the supervisory area and get back in line to get another cue. Most aspiring pool sharks at Austin's real pool halls got their start at Shaw Gym. One of the most distressing sights to me in modern-day Austin is the empty spot where that most revered old building stood.

The last thing I want to remember here is that famous institution of my generation, The Tower. Some involved parents decided, correctly, that kids needed a place to let off steam under adult supervision, so they purchased and renovated a second- story series of rooms above George's

Pizza Parlor. The main room had a wonderful hardwood floor, and because it was on the second story, it had just enough spring to make a perfect dance floor.

With a snack bar and tables, occasional live music, and the excellent jukebox music of the era, the Tower was an institution for teenagers of the entire area, not just Austin. A particular style of dancing evolved there, and no matter if you were in Owatonna, Albert Lea, Rochester, or anywhere else in southern Minnesota, you could immediately recognize someone from Austin, or at least the Tower, by the way he or she danced. The stairway to the second story was wide and open, with a landing half way up. I will never forget the rush of anticipation I felt as the music cascaded and echoed down that stairway, meeting us on our way in.

It strikes me that my friends and I truly had a good place to grow up--as much as some of us have grown up anyway. It may seem that we lacked parental supervision, but that is part of the point. We neither wanted nor NEEDED much, and never suffered for lack of it. My parents, as well as those of my friends, invariably asked pointedly where we were going, with whom, and when we would be back. Satisfied on those points, they basically cut us loose to go and have a good time. The "soccer mom" concept was unheard of, and I believe we were better off for it.

I don't understand why things have changed so drastically, but they have. Too few parents allow or encourage minimally supervised play, depriving their children of circumstances in which they can develop imagination, social skills, and perseverance. On the other hand, who can blame parents, when every day brings to light some new horror?

I suppose things as they are don't require my understanding or approval. I am certain of one thing: I am both fortunate and grateful for the time and place in which I spent my childhood.

Ole Kookens and More Ole Kookens
by Bonnie Broesder Hauser

My mother and father, Casper and Tena Broesder, came from Holland as children, met around 1920, married in 1923, lived on farms near Lismore and Adrian, and lived many years in Adrian. We six kids looked forward to New Years' Day because that's when Mom made a Dutch delicacy known as Ole Kookens or Ole Bollen.

On New Year's Eve, Mom set the dough--not in a bowl, but in a huge dish pan or even in a wash tub. The dough raised all night, and on New Year's morning, the ritual started. Someone put a huge pot of lard on the stove. We didn't have gas or electricity so we had to start and stoke a good corn cob and wood stove fire to melt and heat all that lard. As soon as the lard heated, which took some time, the frying began.

Why so much dough and lard? This is what we ate all New Year's Day! Spoonfuls of dough were dropped into the hot lard, and when one side was nice and brown, the Ole Kookens turned themselves over to brown the other side. When they were done, we rolled them in sugar. Oh, they were so good eaten hot!

When we got old enough, we kids could make them ourselves, and we had a great time designing different shapes. Ours would have legs or tendrils and resemble animals like octopus or spiders. The house would be covered with blue film from all that hot lard, but we didn't care.

My younger sister Doree still makes Ole Kookens, and they are enjoyed by my two brothers and their families who all live in Adrian. Doree whips up a much smaller batch and a faster version of the recipe. And of course, she has a modern kitchen so she doesn't have to build and tend the fire on the stove.

Each New Year's I wait for a package to arrive in the mail. Yes, my Minnesota sister always sends me a batch of Ole Kookens, and she also sends some to my sister who lives in Denver. Some traditions are just too good to give up.

Ole Kookens

1 quart warm liquid--milk, water or potato water
2 packages yeast
2 1/2 cups sugar
salt
1/2 package currants
8-10 cups of flour

Dissolve yeast in 2 cups warm liquid and let set for 5 minutes. Add 1/2 cup sugar, 2 cups flour, mix so it's like a sponge mix. Add the rest of the water, sugar, salt, currants and flour. The mixture should be sponge-like. Set the mixture in a warm place until it at least doubles in size. Drop by tablespoonfuls into hot fat.

Bonnie Broesder Hauser lives in Iowa City. She sent this story after reading about Minnesota Memories in the Nobles County Review, her hometown paper.

Family Vacations at Camp Damp
by Vicki Nelson

Minnesota summer brings fond memories of family vacations. We were a camping family who loved the outdoors, or at least pretended to. It was a cheap family vacation with the possibility of adventure. I'm sure that as kids we liked camping a lot more than our parents did. We explored parks and places off the beaten trail. We always brought along our fishing equipment, and ingredients for making s'mores, but the biggest thing we almost always brought with us with us was rainy weather.

On one particular trip, we traveled to southwest Minnesota, where we camped on a small lake. From the time we arrived, the clouds just couldn't wait to give us our due. Droplets of rain began coming down. My dad quickly put up our tent, but tents didn't go up as easily then as they do now, and we couldn't get inside quickly enough. We spent that evening in damp clothes and slept in damp sleeping bags.

We awoke to a gorgeous morning. The sun shone brightly, the birds were singing--all welcoming us to a new and glorious day. The tent aired out, and we hung our belongings out to dry. We celebrated our new day with a fishing trip and were having a blast when the sky became dark.

Without waiting for us to get back to shore, the clouds again opened up and dumped buckets of water on our heads. Soaking wet, we stood at our tent and laughed at our lousy luck. It was as if we were rain gods who could make rain by going on a camping trip. Fortunately for us, relatives who lived fairly close by offered us a dry place to spend the night.

I have my own family now, and the camping tradition has continued. And, as always, rain likes to join us when we camp. Minnesota, I hear, has the best storms, and we have experienced many of the finest. At times, I thought we might either get blown away or float away through the park in our tent on the water that gathered beneath us. But I wouldn't trade any of those memories. I look forward to making more camping memories - rain and all!

Vicki Nelson lives in St. Louis Park, where she home-schools one of her two teenage sons. She enjoys writing, reading, cooking, and family time.

Duluth Youth and the Magic of the Northern Lights
by Arthur H. Thompson

When I read about the turmoil in education today, I often think of my own experience in Duluth years ago. I started Washburn School in Hunters Park in 1923, and since I lived out in the country, I was one of a few who rode Mr. Murray's old red bus to the school. We were a rarity at the time, for most children walked from their suburban homes.

Mr. Murray had a hard time in winter, and especially in spring when frost coming out of the ground created sinkholes in the primitive gravel roads. I recall getting stuck several times on the Jean Duluth Road by the Johnson farm, and Mr. Murray walking over to fetch Mr. Johnson and his team of horses to pull us out of the hole.

Despite severe winter weather, the school system did not declare snow days because there was no means of communicating such a decision. No homes had radios in the 20's, nor even in the 30's when I attended high school; radio did not yet broadcast news and weather. Thus, in the severest weather, parents kept children home, but most days were school days regardless of weather.

Washburn School was headed by our principal, Mabel Rossman, and a staff of teachers, all single women who brooked no nonsense. We were disciplined for talking in class, for chewing gum, sometimes for not paying attention. Our teachers were dedicated women, and I remember some of them, including Lucille Hoar, Daisy Grimm, Nellie Cleve, Irma Bergtold, and Margaret Taylor.

We were drilled in all subjects and were well prepared to move on to East Junior High for seventh grade. In the short fall period, we played soccer, of all things, a game I never heard of again until my grandchildren played it in California. Most of the school year, however, we skated on good ice on the playground.

I can still recall the scene, the sounds, and the smell of the warming house at all public rinks. In the short spring, we boys played marbles while the girls played jacks. The best marble player was a boy named Hammerstrom; his parents called him Robert, while we called him "Oola."

East Junior High was a marvelous experience for all of us. The building was nearly new, modern in every way, and situated on a sizeable acreage studded with beautiful birch trees. Mr. Murray had retired, so we now rode with Lloyd Rehbine on a newer Reo bus, likely a 1930 model. The redesigned Jean Duluth Road gave fewer problems, though it was still not paved, and snow removal equipment could now help keep this road open in winter.

The school presented a whole new world complete with shop classes that I enjoyed. I remember Mr. Johnson telling us on opening day of our electricity class not to ask him what electricity is, for he didn't know! Girls emerged as odd characters who did weird things with their faces and hair which I didn't understand. Come to think of it, I still do not understand junior high girls.

After nine years in public schools, I moved on to Cathedral High, a Catholic school for boys. Our school was in a very old building downtown, just two blocks from Duluth Central High--minimal facilities with no embellishments of any kind, and a faculty of Christian Brothers who were second to none in training--and controlling--teenage boys. We were presented with no snap courses, and no options.

I remember Brother John opening all windows for a few minutes at the beginning of English class, even when the temperature was well below zero outside. He said the fresh air would keep us awake--and it did.

Brother Edward was the best of several history teachers, while Brother Patrick, a young Irishman from Chicago, was a tough but brilliant math teacher. When we received a diploma, it meant something, and although all of us were well-prepared for college level work, few of us in the desperate Depression would ever get to college.

Cathedral boys came from all over the city, and I remember some of them very well. Si Forgette was our class humorist, Dick "Leather Lung" Foggarty our cheerleader. Dick could out-yell any stand of fans at a football game, and I often wondered if he ever used his capability later as a lawyer in court. John "Nose" Mahoney was one of that memorable foursome in Woodland which included Nose, Satchel, Cut and Meadows.

We had almost no extracurricular activities, because our building was on nothing but a city lot just uphill from the center of the city.

There were no proms at Cathedral, but we did have a senior class picnic one Saturday at Caribou Lake with lots to eat-- a real treat we appreciated. We did have some athletes, and they won the conference championship in my junior year in both football and basketball, which required a playoff game with Denfeld High in Central's gym. I had to walk to and from the trolley terminal that night, but I watched our team win 27-16. That score is almost unbelievable today, but back then, each basketball field goal was followed by a center jump to resume play.

When I enrolled at Cathedral, I was no longer eligible to ride on the public school bus that had been my transportation for nine years. I got a ride on a cream truck each morning to a suburban dairy where I caught a trolley downtown. In the afternoon, I rode the trolley to the end of the line at Woodland and walked home from there.

It was a three and a half mile hike, a trial for some, but actually therapy for me. I developed severe abdominal pains in grade school, so severe that by the sixth grade, I was convinced I did not have long to live. The problem was diagnosed soon thereafter as a duodenal ulcer, and by the time I got to high school, my internist ordered a daily hike of at least two miles regardless of what else I did that day. Thus, my walk was ulcer therapy, and fortunately, I like to walk.

I remember that walk well even today--the cemetery just out of Woodland, the Eastbound leg upgrade through Greysolon, the view of Lake Superior from the top of Murdock's Hill. When I got to the bottom of that long hill, I reached Jean Duluth Road. I now had 3/4 mile to go-- due north. When the temperature was well below zero, as it often was, and the wind was whistling out of the northwest, I walked most of that distance backward to keep my face from freezing. I thought nothing of it, but now the thought makes me shudder.

I walked home in the dark much of the school year, and it was then I was introduced to the amazing night sky, with constellations punctuated by the spectacular aurora borealis, the northern lights. It was a vast outdoor theater with a beautiful sparkling ceiling and the ever-changing shape and color of illumination coming from the north. I was enchanted with it all, and even now I reflect at times on the allure of a winter night in northern Minnesota.

I graduated from Cathedral High School on a Friday night in 1936 and enrolled Monday morning at Duluth State Teachers College to take a summer session course in botany. I had but one weekend between high school and college, and during the nine years of my collegiate work (undergraduate and graduate school), I reflected at times on how well the academic rigor of Cathedral High prepared me for what was to follow.

On my nightly ulcer hike later at the University of Minnesota, I was shut out from the heavenly scene I knew was there by all the lights of the Twin Cities, and I missed it. Indeed, after high school I was never again to enjoy that sensational show that had so touched my life. I regarded it as a bit of magic; I still do.

Arthur Thompson, retired professor of pomology at University of Maryland, lives in Catonville, Maryland. An avid reader, he enjoys cultivating different varieties of azaleas. He was prompted to write this story after his daughter Janet sent him a copy of the first volume of Minnesota Memories.

Alice and Me
by Maria Murad

I spent a lot of weekends with my aunt Alice, my mother's older sister. Alice never married, but she knew how children's minds worked. Hers was the steady hand that guided me through the murky depths of my childhood.

One of my favorite memories is Sundays at Alice's. At home, I hated going to church, but with Alice it was different. Her little church was St. Stephen's on 4th Avenue near the Minneapolis Art Institute. Even then, so many years ago, that church was old and drafty and smelled of linseed polish. But the stained glass windows and colorful statues fascinated me.

No plain white ceramic Mary inhabited this church; she was done up in blues and golds and greens. The statue of the Infant of Prague had a real cloth outfit, white satin with gold braid and sparkly accents. Even the Missions were fun. While the visiting priest preached about sin and hell, I fingered a glorious rosary box Alice bought me. In the flickering candlelight, the box looked as if it were encrusted with real rubies, and I inhaled the exotic scent of incense like some Sybarite.

Alice was very religious, and from the time I was small, every Holy Thursday we pilgrimaged across the Twin Cities by streetcar to visit all the churches we possibly could. I recall vaguely that a faithful Catholic stored up indulgences this way.

I loved going with her, boarding yellow streetcars with their straw-patterned seats. The streetcars made a great racket as they charged down the middle of the streets on their metal rails. Sometimes the trolley cable went off its track above the car with an explosion of sparks. The conductor would stop the car, get off, and using a long pole would put the cable back in place with admirable speed. The job complete, he would then swing back up to his seat and move forward.

I always got to deposit tokens and ask for transfers. I think we could traverse both cities on one token and lots of transfers.

What an odd pair we were--she with her hennaed red hair, me with my straight black hair done up temporarily in curls she'd set in rags the night before. Her high heels raced swiftly up and down church aisles, while I followed breathlessly with short, fat legs in Mary Jane sandals. With abandon we lit votive candles in shimmering containers --blue, red, gold--leaving behind countless prayers in countless churches in Minneapolis and St. Paul.

We remained buddies, allies really, all during my growing-up years, although our excursions changed a bit. Because I was interested in theater and dance, she took me to stage shows at the Orpheum in downtown Minneapolis, and shopping trips and visits by train to Duluth relatives, and on my 18th birthday, we journeyed to St. Petersburg, Florida.

She loved traveling around the country, often alone by bus. Until she retired, she was a Chief Operator for the Bell Telephone Company, with her own little house at 1921 Clinton at the corner of 4th and Clinton. That house is long gone, bulldozed away, but curiously, it looks familiar and comforting to me when I drive by. The Windsor apartments are still catty-corner from it, and the old houses across the street still stand.

So many memories, so many good things stored up in my heart. My aunt Alice stood between me and the unhappiness of my childhood, whether real or imagined. My mother was, I think now, unstable, a mercurial woman who blew hot and cold in her approval and disapproval of her children. Alice took me away, indulged me, listened to me, called me "Sugar" and kept me on some kind of path.

Her religious attitude was practical and encompassed her life, and that legacy has stood me in good stead. She didn't talk much about God and the saints, but evidence of her faith was everywhere, from the scapular she wore around her neck to the huge picture of the Sacred Heart prominently hung on her wall in the living room of that little house.

With sadness I watched as small strokes eroded her sharpness, her brightness, her quickness, and finally left her bedridden and uncomprehending. On my wedding day, I went to her nursing home and laid my bouquet in her hands. I fancied there was a brief recognition in her green eyes as I kissed her cheek.

She died soon after, never seeing my children, whom she would have adored. She was buried from her beloved St. Stephen's, and I sat with my first child on my lap, reliving the sounds and smells and vibrations that echoed in that familiar place.

She loved traveling around the country, often alone by bus.

Maria B Murad is a freelance writer and editor who loves to dance, travel, and spend time with her three gorgeous grandchildren. She lives with her husband George in Apple Valley

Head, Heart, Hands and Health
by Arvin Rolfs

While reading the 1999 County Fair edition of the Rock County Star Herald, I was disappointed to learn that my old 4-H club, the North Star, no longer exists. Just as disappointing was to learn that another club my family had been involved with, The Kenneth Hustlers, was not even mentioned in that article as ever having existed!

It's not surprising that a small youth group like a 4-H club would extinguish over fifty years, but I always expected that all those meeting minutes we sent in to the County Extension Office over the years would be kept for posterity. There was information in those mandatory minutes, attendance, demonstrations given, awards received, etc. that I thought would be recorded forever. Apparently not! Not only are individual achievements forever lost to collective memory, but even the existence of these clubs and their social value have been lost to time.

In this contribution to *Minnesota Memories*, I would like to share my recollections of these two clubs, the people involved, and their contributions to Kenneth and the surrounding community.

A danger of any one person's recollections is that there are bound to be lapses of memory where people are left off a list, or where names or deeds are attributed to the wrong people. For these imperfections I apologize, but I feel it is important to tell stories and risk an offense.

My preschool memory of The Kenneth Hustlers is tied mainly to the activities of my two older brothers, Leonard and Dean.. What they did and who they did it with are the things I best remember. The Ingolf Sunde family was the single largest contributor to the group with Ruth, Avis, Eileen, Bernard, Ralph and David all being members at some time or other. The Gilbert Remme family was probably next with Virgil, Vivian and Elwood as members. Erling and Luther Severtson were also very active in the club while my brothers were involved. Other names that come to my mind now have only fuzzy faces to accompany them: Delores Gullickson, VerJoyce and Alice Buss, Norm Anderson,who died from polio in '46 or '47. These were the people who mentored my brothers in their 4-H experiences. These were big kids I admired from a distance.

I probably never knew why the club folded and hardly remember when it did, but it wasn't long until our parents got us involved in another club, The North Star. This was the club that became my club when I was 9 years old in 1948.

It was an amazing thing how becoming a member of this group changed my status among these new big kids from being a nobody to being one of them. The very night I joined, I was included in the game activities as a full-fledged member, and I interacted with teenagers as an equal; whereas a month earlier I could just as easily have gotten smacked for daring to speak to one of them!

This was classic group dynamics, and it was great! In this club were kids my age to relate to, kids older to learn from, and adults willing to help me fit in. The families that comprised this club were from east of Hardwick, with the Emil Peterson kids: Lee, Lois and Loryn, the Art Cooksley family: Lois, Darrell and Dan; Don and Ron Haaman, and the Eldo Strassberg boys. I don't remember their names anymore, except for Junior, who was my age and died later that same year from polio.

The North Star was a more active club that participated with other clubs in county-wide activities. In fact, I joined just in time to take part in a humorous one-act play contest held at the Magnolia High School gym. Our play depicted some lively conversations among several unenlightened fans at an exciting football game, and I was privileged to play someone in the cheering section. I still remember my lines: "Rah! Rah! Rah!, Shish! Boom! Bah!" Our play didn't win, but from the fun of seeing other plays and the excitement of being part of the effort, I felt I had won a lot.

This was just the frosting however. The meat and potatoes, the reason for being in 4-H in the first place, was our projects. My two brothers started out in the Kenneth club with the basic three: poultry, gardening and home beautification, which represented most of their chores at home. But what made the North Star experience the big leagues for them, as well as for me, was our hog project.

Of course it was not fair to them that a 9- year- old rookie started out at the same level as my two 4-H hardened, teenaged brothers, but I never heard any real complaint from them. Our parents were of the opinion we were all in this together so Dad picked out three gilts for us to raise, separate from the rest of the herd.

I was the major benefactor from this hog project. While Leonard and Dean were out in the field helping Dad put up hay, or walking the corn and beans, hoeing thistles or pulling up cockleburs, I was in the hog pen, hand-feeding or grooming the gilts, developing a personal relationship with them. They came to identify me with feeling good, which was a big boost to my self-esteem.

Eventually I learned that 4-H was not all play; there was real grunt work involved with these projects. Just three weeks before the county fair, we were notified that our project records were due at the extension office in Luverne. What a reality check! I learned after only a few years of agonizing over this task that records were supposed to be an ongoing report of progress, a tool to help manage the project, not a tool of torture nor a creative writing process. But for the first year, these finer points of project management did not register strongly with me.

What did register with me were the many questions that encouraged very long answers. "Additional pages may be used," written after each question was not reassuring. I was an advocate of the short answer - one word or less, but my mother would have none of that. The written results of my hours of staring at empty pages and the final intervention of my parents would have been a worthy candidate for the pages of *Successful Farming*, but it certainly did not portray my projects my way. But no matter! I was not after the Grand Champion ribbon for records. The records were done and turned in. I was a qualified exhibitor, and nothing could keep me and my pig from the county fair.

Except polio...!!

I never understood how my brothers managed and maintained our exhibits at the fair while our parents stayed with me at the Sister Kenny Institute in Minneapolis during fair time, but they did. Nor did I ever know what price their pigs brought at the auction following the fair. I suspect my pig brought out the sympathy bid at $6.66 per pound. Considering today's prices, 1948 certainly must have been the good old days.

When I returned from the hospital a year later, the North Star was a far different club. Attrition from age and high school activities culled out the Peterson, Cooksley, Haaman and Strassburg families, leaving my two brothers, Donald and Dorothy Kindt, Dale Strassburg, and myself as the remaining members. At election time there were just enough officer positions to go around, with one member at large. I was elected song leader because Dale turned the job down first. Dean assumed that job along with the presidency because he knew I could never lead a song anywhere, even with a rope and halter.

A short time later our cousin Darwin Erickson joined the club. His sister Sandy, my younger brother Dave, and Dale's brother Delmar, would be eligible for membership in a few years so we had some hope. But my mother, recognizing that to be a viable club we would have to expand our membership, began to canvass the community for potential candidates.

She found many people just waiting to be asked. At its peak during my involvement, the club could boast of the above members plus Doris, Loryn, and Sherrie Ask, Yvonne and Vivian Atkinson, Gordon and Linda Funk, the Walt Halverson family, Louise, Adella, Phyllis, Stan, Margaret, Arnie and Gary; Ken and Kathy Hoime, Charlotte, Marjorie and Karin Huisman, LeRoy Oldre, Roger and Larry Tweet and Veralyn and Evan VerSteeg. 4-H took over the neighborhood, impacting even our home when my mother invited the girls over once a week so that she could help them with their sewing projects.

My own projects took on a different profile. Since I no longer could manage a hog project, my parents encouraged me to find projects I could manage and relate to. There were two that redefined 4-H for me: raising rabbits and wildlife conservation.

The success of these projects may be questioned by some, but my personal benefit was denied by none. Raising rabbits was not as easy as many believe, particularly among my breed of choice. Angoras turned out to be as temperamental as they are furry. Profits from their double assets of meat and fur were far more elusive than ads in the small stock magazines led me to believe.

Angora fur was a desired commodity by few buyers, but only in pound units. To imagine how much thistle down weighs a pound is to envision how long it took to accumulate a pound of Angora rabbit fur. And before considering the market value of a delectable rabbit drummie, I had to factor how much less fur that drummie would contribute forever after. My rabbit project was not a financial success, but it kept me involved.

And so did my wildlife conservation project. I can imagine now how my mother must have felt, watching me throughout the winter inching through snowdrifts on my crutches out to the grove with a big bag of oats over one shoulder and ear corn over the other to replenish my feeding stations, but she never hinted I should stop doing it or that one of my brothers could do it for me.

I can imagine that a farmer could view boarding a flock of pheasants through the winter and contributing hills of corn to them in the spring as having a possible payoff when some of those ringnecks show up at home on his dinner table in October. But there is absolutely no payoff to a farmer who harbors a family of raccoons that found my wood lot habitat inviting. My father did his best to discourage their raids on the hen house, but he never suggested I switch to a different project or maybe focus on songbirds instead.

Maybe county agent Greg Luehr had those considerations in mind when he awarded me the Conservation Prize at the annual award banquet at the Armory that autumn of 1953. From my perspective, he made an excellent choice and got two winners that year - the alternate who went to Conservation Camp and I, who got a pin and glory!

That was my last year of active involvement in 4-H, although I continued vicariously for several more years through my brother Dave's participation. In those years though, I could see a hint of how the North Star's success could also lead to its demise. During the height of the club's membership, some parents began voicing misgivings about hosting their turn at the monthly meetings, which were family affairs with total turnout from 25 to 50 hungry, often boisterous people. The club was permitted to renovate the basement of Kenneth Grade School, which in 1952 became the club's permanent meeting place, and the meeting place for other community groups as well.

However, as using the school reduced the hosting requirements of all parents, it also seemed to reduce their involvement. For more and more kids the school became a drop-off place. And with fewer parents attending meetings, things became more unruly. Instead of organized activities for kids after the meeting, kids were let outside to expel their energy harmlessly. Control was left entirely to the adult leaders, rather than shared by all parents as it had been.

With that progression, I am not surprised that The North Star dissolved. What surprises me is that more clubs have not. Maybe there is something to be learned about social behavior by comparing the clubs that have survived with those that have not. I believe survival of a youth group is totally dependent on parents who care enough to give of themselves. I am so grateful that mine, Walter and Norma (Arp) Rolfs, did just that.

Arvin Rolfs taught Spanish and German in Bird Island and Elkton, S. D. He is now a computer systems analyst and lives in Brooklyn Center.

18 U.S.C. 707

The Prize Pony
by Rich Geary

We were seniors that year, 1961, at Owatonna High School. Bob, Jess, Dave, and I ran together a lot-- duck hunting, pheasant hunting and goose hunting on Mussman's farm, bowling, hanging out-- the kind of things high school friends do.

We were not especially interested in Southern Minne League baseball, but when Jess' mother Vera offered us free tickets for the game at Darts Park, we decided to go. I guess it was more a sense of being together that last year. We knew we would all be going our separate ways after graduation so it was some time to spend together.

We knew they were giving away a Shetland pony at the game. Mrs. Bredlow called Mother and wanted her son and my brother Bob to go to the game, but Mom said no, with our luck Bob would probably win the pony. I remember walking by it when we were going to our seats. I even remember calling it a nag.

Dave had a real look of terror in his eyes when he heard his last name being called; he thought he had won the horse. It turned out to be his cousin winning something else. We had a good laugh about that. Then it happened; they called my name as winner of the horse. I tried to duck, but my good friends made me go down and get my prize pony.

"Why don't you ride him?" suggested someone as he handed me the reins.

"Yeah, I guess I could."

As I put my foot in the stirrup and slid into the new black saddle with silver trappings, I sure hoped he wouldn't buck me off in front of all those people. There may have been other classmates in the stands. I was a senior, after all.

Now what would I do? I guessed I would probably have to ride this horse all the way home. But I had driven that night. Well, Bob, it looks like you will have to drive the green Plymouth to my house.

Some guy came up to me and offered me $35 for the horse. I was tempted, but I figured the saddle was worth that much. Looking back, I should have taken the cash.

It was a long ride to Hillcrest Avenue on the other side of town. And, much to my surprise, there waiting for me in the doorway were my parents, in their night clothes. At 10:45 Nelder Olson with Alexander Lumber Company, a competitor of my Dad, who worked for United Building Center, called him to ask if he could bid on our new horse barn.

"Nelder, what are you talking about? Isn't it past your bedtime?"

Looking out the window by the phone, Dad could see me and the pony rounding the corner on Truman Avenue and Phelps Street, slowly plodding towards home.

We kept the pony tied to a cement block in the vacant lot next to the house. A neighbor called Mom the next morning and said she sat down in the bathroom and then jumped up again when she looked out the window and saw the pony-- not believing her eyes. She said she was up and down for the next five minutes. I spent the better part of the next week giving all the neighborhood kids pony rides.

About three days after I won the pony, Dad got a personal visit from the County Sheriff. He wanted to know if I had won a pony and where it was. The fast talking promoter who convinced the Medford farmer to sell the pony for the raffle had given the farmer a rubber check and was now nowhere to be found.

"That's not our problem," said Dad. "My son won the horse, and he's going to keep it." So much for my second chance to ditch the pony.

As much as the neighborhood kids wanted Sheldon the pony to stay in the lot, we found that if we joined the Saddle Club, we could board him at the Steele County Fair Grounds. And that is where he spent the summer. He needed riding and exercising, and the race track was the ideal place for that. Sheldon soon figured out that as soon as he was half way around the track, he was headed for home, so he always galloped the last half of the track.

We had to move Sheldon from the horse barn for the Steele County Free Fair, and Larry LaRue had a farm on the edge of town where he let us keep Sheldon. Apparently we should have checked this arrangement with Sheldon first. We got a call; Sheldon had broken his halter and was back at the fairgrounds eating grass, so I had to go over there and deal with the situation.

My life as a cowboy and horse wrangler soon came to a close. About the time I headed off for the University of Minnesota, the salesman from Pegg Ford caught Dad in a mood for a trade. Dad's last words before closing the deal were, "Oh by the way, take a Shetland Pony and the deal is done." We traded Sheldon in for a '57 Chevrolet.

Rich Geary earned a BS in Forestry at the University of Minnesota. He markets forest products in Southern California and sails his 30' boat in San Diego Bay and the Pacific Ocean.

My brother poses with Sheldon, the Prize Pony.

1951 Atwater Winter
by Marion Field

It was an unusual winter. By February 26, 1951, we had not had any snow. Dirt blew in onto the window sills. We were moving from north of Kandiyohi to Peter Larson's farm about a quarter of a mile from the southwest shore of Diamond Lake. Our new address would be Atwater, Route 2.

The people moving off this place were getting a new fuel tank at their new place so they offered to sell us their old one, which still had a little fuel oil in it. They also had a thirty gallon drum of fuel on a wood rack for an emergency which they agreed to leave for us.

Several friends with trucks helped us move on February 27. We had to move twelve milk cows, pigs, silage, ground feed, hay, straw, and household items. We had our John Deere tractor there in the machine shed. The other machinery we decided to leave at the old place for a few days.

When we loaded furniture on the trucks, we loaded the linoleum that covered the floors last, rolled up loosely, tied with twine, and placed carefully on top of the furniture so it wouldn't get cracked or crushed. The linoleums were then handy to unload first and lay on the floors before we put down stoves, beds and other furniture.

Once we were into the new place, we got our stoves up and going. The beds were next, and we made them up so we would have a place to sleep. We barely got settled that Friday when it started to snow. We fed, milked, and bedded the cows early. We had a galvanized tank with cold water in it to cool the milk. We had a large cistern by the windmill that was piped to the barn for the cows' drinking cups.

The next morning, still tired from the big move, we had to get the animals fed, the cows milked and bedded, and the manure cleaned up from behind the cows. We had to carry feed and water to the pigs. It was hard physical labor. While we worked, more snow fell.

As the day wore on, snow kept falling and falling! The wind came up and blew relentlessly. We had a good blizzard that kept on and on. About noon the next day, the oil burners in the house went out. We weren't too concerned because we knew we had the extra thirty gallon barrel out by the big tank on a wood rack to be used for just such emergencies.

Marvin went out to get some fuel from the thirty gallon barrel and got an unpleasant surprise.   Oh, no! The wood rack had broken, and the barrel had fallen on its lever and drained all the fuel onto the ground.

What to do? We called our neighbors, Orbin and Grace Rear, to see if they had any extra fuel. Yes, they said they had plenty, and Marvin should come over and get some. Our tractor was too snowed in by then to get it out of the machine shed. We didn't have a snow scoop for that tractor anyway. There was far too much snow for one person to start shoveling by hand.

It seemed that the only alternative was for Marvin to take two five gallon cans and walk across the fields to Rears' farm, which was at least a mile away. I didn't think Marvin should take two five gallon cans because they would be too heavy, but he thought it would be easier to balance two.

Orbin and Grace were having afternoon coffee when Marvin got there. They insisted that he have some lunch with them and rest a little before he started for home. They would not have it any other way. That was good because Marvin needed the rest!

At chore time I looked out across the fields and could not see Marvin coming through the blowing snow.   I knew how tired he would be when he got home. The house was starting to get cold.

I dressed 4-year-old Michael and 2-year-old James warmly. I had James stand on a chair, and I sat on the edge of the chair so he could climb onto my back, and I told Michael to hang on tightly to my coat. I pushed snow away with my arms, and we got to the barn-- but I still could not see Marvin coming across the field.

I fed the cows their silage and ground feed that was all in the old silage room. When that was done, I started to milk. Now I could finally see Marvin coming, but he was still quite a distance away. I just finished milking when he made it to the barn at last. Oh, I was so glad to see him! He put the fuel cans down and rested awhile.

Marvin told me how his eyes kept freezing shut and how heavy wet snow and wind had tried to push him back. He had to put the cans down several times so that he could put his hands over his eyes and mouth and blow warm air on his face to reopen his eyes.

Marvin took the fuel to the house. He started the stoves and waited to see that they were going good. While he was waiting he called Orbin and Grace to thank them again for the fuel and to let them know that he made it home safely. It had been terrible for him.

Marvin came back down to the barn then. I was done washing up the milkers. He loaded the ten gallon cans of milk into the cooling tank and bedded the cows. Then we fed, watered, and bedded the pigs. We had to carry everything. Later that evening the wind started to calm down, and we all went to bed exhausted!

The next morning the wind was still, and the snow had stopped falling. The snow plow went by early in the morning so we were able to get the fuel truck out and have the big tank filled again. The milk truck also got there and picked up our milk.

I don't know what we would have done if Marvin hadn't had so much stamina. This was the first blizzard we had that year, and we had a blizzard every weekend in March. It was the unusual winter of 1951, a year I won't forget.

Marion Field is a retired farm wife and family biographer who lives in Litchfield. Her son Mike encouraged her to send this story.

Perfect Morning at River Valley
by Gene Grazzini Jr.

The alarm goes off at 5:00. I get up slowly and take care of my morning duties, let Gusto do his thing, and kennel him up. We're off to meet my favorite hunting partner. Last night the rain came down in buckets. We had agreed the evening before that if it was raining in the morning, we would call it off. This morning is overcast, but it isn't raining.

We are set to meet at the Lion's Tap parking lot at 6:00. I pull in five minutes early. Greg has his window open on the Chevy truck, and Bombay, standing in the pickup box, greets me as I pull in.

Greg mumbles, "G'morning. I been here since quarter to five."
I ask him why, and he says, "I couldn't sleep."
I say, "Good to know you can still get excited over hunting."

I pull in front of him, and we proceed down to the bottoms. The chain is down, so we drive right through. The road going downhill appears to have washed out with last night's rains so I keep my fingers crossed that the rest of the road is okay. I shouldn't have worried; the road is fine.

In the inky blackness I find the corn swathe I marked yesterday while hunting with Joe Monahan. I have to finish my morning duties in the field while Greg continues his usual hunting morning ritual. We proceed out into the soaking wet field, sinking to our ankles as we tote our decoys out, trying to walk on downed corn stalks. Both dogs kick up mud running after each other, snarling and growling-- just their usual greeting. Ducks are working our field like kamikazes; flock after flock buzzes us; even a small flock of geese try to get into our decoys while we're back at the car getting our guns and shells.

By 6:20 we've got our decoys set, and we're standing in the towering corn stalks waiting for our first flight of honkers. We can hear them on Rice Lake north of us. Sunup is at 6:50, and we don't see many flocks moving. When they start to move, Greg is calling on his goose call and I'm calling on mine. I expect any moment to hear his usual warning to quit calling because I'm scaring the birds. We work a small flock in, knock two down, and Greg is mumbling to himself that he's shooting behind the birds. Bombay attempts to retrieve one bird, then switches off that bird to get the other one. Bombay's probably a little rusty.

In the lull between flocks, I ask Greg to tell Maureen that today's the day for the baby to be born. The 12th was my pick in the baby pool.

We both continue to call, and the birds continue to come, but we're set up wrong for the wind. Wind is out of the west, and we're standing in the corn to the east of our decoys, which means the birds have to fly over our cornstalks to land in our decoys. However, we're able to get them working to our stool-- even with the wrong wind. And then I hear a startling statement from my number one son.

"Dad, hit 'em again with your call." I thought I'd have to go to my grave without hearing those words.

We stop a moment to count birds, making sure we don't go over the limit. We've got eight beautiful Canadians down. We need two to fill our limit. We settle back into the cornstalks as a triple heads our way out of the west. We're on the calls as the birds zero in on our decoys. As they swing over us, Greg says, "You take the right; I'll take the left."

Two shots ring out as the bird on the left drops out of flight. A second later the right bird tumbles out. The middle bird continues on unscathed. We've limited out together on called shots. A perfect morning shoot. It's 7:15.

We struggle out to the road with decoys, guns, and possible's bags. Then we go back to the field as we each string five geese to a dog leash sling. We hoist the birds to our shoulders and trudge towards the road as Greg observes, "This is the hardest part of the shoot."

It's 7:55 as we take our leave of the River Valley Hunt Club. Time to go to church. We've had a truly perfect morning.

Gene Grazzini is a Burnsville terrazzo, marble, granite and ceramic tile contractor who has been writing about his hunting and fishing trips for 25 years.

Hungarian Catholic? What Kind of Husband is That?
By Kathy Megyeri

Raised a good Lutheran in Owatonna and graduating from St. Olaf College in Northfield, I was always expected to marry one of my own kind. But in 1963, I had the good fortune to attend a summer school session in Washington, D. C., and seated beside me in a class at George Washington University was the most continental, sophisticated, smartest person I had ever met. Unfortunately, he was Catholic and Hungarian!

At the time, however, his religion and nationality didn't really matter to me because we were just dating. We attended such exciting and historical events together-- Barry Goldwater Presidential nomination rally at the D.C. National Guard Armory, Martin Luther King's "I Have A Dream" speech on the steps of the Lincoln Memorial, and our first date which was a canoe trip down the Potomac River to attend a Watergate concert.

Particularly memorable was the fact that after paddling for an hour, this continental and sophisticated date told me not to turn around. I heard a tinkle of water as he discreetly peed over the side. Fortunately, it was dark, and canoeists on either side never paid any attention to us.

After those heady and memorable summer days, I returned home to Minnesota, and he started law school in Washington. We corresponded, and he even drove cross-country to visit me over Thanksgiving the next year. My dad, a private pilot at the time, took him up in his airplane, flew him over St. Olaf College, and informed him that a good Lutheran from St. Olaf would be the most perfect husband for his daughter--a hint that he should disappear from the radar scope.

My mother, confusing Hungary with Honduras, bought him bunches of bananas, assuming they would be his favorite snack. He accepted the bananas but patiently explained that Honduras and Hungary are continents apart, and that he didn't speak Spanish. When the courtship and letters continued, my parents started to worry. It didn't impress them that after obtaining his law degree, he attained a CPA and an MBA. What really mattered was that he was Hungarian and Catholic!

Following graduation, I took a teaching job outside Washington, D.C., and five years later, we were married by both a Lutheran minister and a Hungarian priest in a Washington, D.C. Lutheran church.

We both remember the elaborate preparations for such an event because of the permissions we had to obtain, and we still chuckle over the pre-marriage counseling sessions during which we were warned of two qualities that would probably tear our marriage apart--cultural and religious differences. However, 32 years later, we are still together--he with his Hungarian accent, me with my Minnesota accent,. We trade off each Sunday between Catholic and Lutheran church services, but we are living proof that such differences can coexist and even flourish.

What is historically most interesting to me is Minnesota's response to the Hungarian Revolution in 1956, which created almost 200,000 refugees, one of whom was to become my husband.

Under Governor Orville L. Freeman, Minnesotans eagerly initiated and participated in relief efforts. They sent aid to survivors in Hungary, they arranged to bring refugees to the United States, they offered them homes and jobs in Minnesota, and they helped them learn English and adjust to life in the North Star State.

The Council for the Liberation of Captive Peoples from Soviet Domination was founded in the Twin Cities, and rallies were held on the steps of the state capitol led by Antal Dorati, director of the Minnesota Symphony Orchestra and a Hungarian who arrived in the United States. in 1941.

The Governor's Committee for Refugee Relief planned for Minnesota to accept 500 to 600 Hungarian refugees, and one radio broadcast alone brought 200 letters promising homes and jobs for dentists, farm hands, factory workers and specialists. Jeno Paulucci, President of Chun King Sales and Wilderness Valley Farms in Duluth, offered his company's facilities and heavy equipment should Hungarian farmers want to settle and grow vegetables in the area, but not many applied because most of the Freedom Fighters, or displaced persons, were urban residents who moved to urban areas like Cleveland, Ohio, and New Brunswick, New Jersey.

In March of 1957, only one hundred thirty Hungarians settled in Minnesota, despite the state's widespread support. Only eight Hungarians found their way to Steele County, where I grew up. Thus, it was no surprise that my family's first introduction to this ethnic group occurred the day I brought my future husband home from college.

I accepted their surprise and skepticism as a challenge.   I had to prove that Lutherans and Catholics can coexist, and more importantly, I had to prove to my parents that a union between a German-American Minnesotan and a Hungarian American immigrant would last--and fortunately, it has.

Kathy Megyeri, who lives in Maryland, was co-author of Minnesota Memories, Volume I. She has contributed articles to numerous publications, and presented sessions for the National Council of Teachers of English national conventions. She taught high school English for thirty-five years.

1939 Eureka Summer
by Robert Montrose

For six of us who had completed another school year, it was a time of celebration in Eureka, a settlement of ten dozen souls two miles west of the more widely known town of Excelsior.   Miss Trumble, our teacher, had determined that we had met certain standards of adequacy, if not excellence, and had therefore promoted us to the next grade.   Our other two classmates, however, would remain behind when we entered grade seven in the fall at Minnewashta Grade School.

Construction of an addition to our school was underway. A library and gymnasium promised new opportunities and activities in the coming year, but for now it was of little interest. It was the summer of 1939 in Eureka, three months of vacation, recreation, and part-time jobs.

Despite conditions which at times appeared to border on mere subsistence, there was no sense of being poor. Only one family in Eureka fell into the needy category, and even they survived without any public subsidies. Adult males with a trade or special talent were, for the most part, employed, earning from a dollar to fifty cents an hour. Summer jobs at fast food places were far in the future, but we kids did what we could to earn some money that summer--even though we were only 11 or 12 years old.

Of the available options, picking berries was the least desired because the pay was low and the conditions were bad. Mowing lawns was sought by boys and some adults. Eureka families mowed their own yards, but Lake Minnetonka with all its monied residents was nearby, so that is where we went. A hard worker could mow as many as three lawns a day, and at twenty-five cents an hour or fifty cents per lawn, there was money to be made.

In 1939 the water table around Eureka was approximately a hundred feet higher than today, so there were many low, marshy areas and a multitude of frogs. Collecting frogs for resale to the fishing resorts provided an enjoyable means of extra income.

Every community seems to have its local character, and ours was a shabbily dressed older fellow we called Turtle Smith. Nobody knew his real name or where he lived, but he hung around the store and made it known that he would pay a quarter for a good sized live turtle. He seemed especially pleased when someone brought him a snapper that measured over a foot across.

Another source of income involved the Minnetonka Country Club. Although this club had been open to golfers for some time, the course needed considerable work. My grandfather, who had used part of that land as a pasture, discovered a problem with the property. The far south edge was comprised of peat covered by a think layer of topsoil. Since peat is a form of fuel, it often catches fire when lightning strikes, and some of these fires burn underground and smolder for years.

Although everything appeared normal on the surface, large underground cavities sometimes swallowed my grandfather's cattle. Years later, when the golf course was constructed on that land, parts of it felt like walking on a sponge. At considerable expense, the club excavated a large area, put out the fires, and filled the holes with soil.

My sister and I lived with our grandparents, the Buchanans, whose house was only a putt away from the seventh fairway. The seventh tee was behind a hill, and errant shots often ended in our small front yard, since there was no buffering area or rough. Some players acted embarrassed as they returned their balls to the fairway, while others insisted on hitting the ball from our lawn, which they seemed to regard as a nuisance that had gotten in their way.

In 1939 golfers either carried their own bags or hired a caddy, since golf carts had not been invented. Without a speedy means of transportation, those caught in a rainstorm either sought shelter under a tree or played on in the rain. A group of such golfers inspired an enterprise.

On a particular Saturday in early June the sky darkened quickly and a light rain began to fall. A foursome on the seventh fairway thought they would tough it out, since the clubhouse was at the opposite side of the course. Suddenly rain turned to hail--pea size at first and rapidly increasing to marble size and larger.

The players, who realized this was more than they had bargained for, dropped their bags and sprinted for the shelter of a large oak tree. The hail increased to the size of golf balls, and even more remarkable was the pure white color of the hail.

As the hail stopped, we watched and laughed as the golfers ventured forth, only to be confronted with tens of thousands of potential golf balls. They could not find their golf balls, and if they played a new ball they would not be able to find it amidst the sea of impostors. They had no choice but to pick up their bags and call it a day. By evening the hail had melted, and I had no trouble adding four balls to my collection.

As players learned the course, and the club installed a buffer, intrusions became less frequent. This presented me with a business opportunity. From the front yard, I could easily see where shots that left the fairway landed in the tall, unmowed grass. At the end of each day, I found a half dozen or more balls, which I sold to players the following day. Spaulding and Wilson brands commanded the best price, and I discovered other locations where a hook or slice almost always resulted in a lost ball.

Course management strongly disapproved of my enterprise because they said I was trespassing. Of course, they hoped to sell those balls or new balls themselves. Caddy masters and maintenance workers chased me whenever they could. If I managed to get outside the course boundaries, I was home free. However, getting caught involved a tongue lashing, a kick in the posterior, a lost cache, or all three. Although my pursuers were older and somewhat quicker, I was skilled at calculating their approaching rate and the distance to the nearest sanctuary. I think both sides enjoyed this pursuit, and I usually got away.

Not all summer activities involved earning money. By mid-June the lakes were warm enough to swim in. After we completed our chores or our jobs, we met at the store to select an activity or swimming hole for the day. A mile to the north was Minnetonka with several nice beaches. A like distance to the south was Lake Minnewashta with its large swimming raft, but also its muddy beach and leeches. Whatever the choice, a half dozen boys and girls were ready for whatever the day would bring.

The long days allowed plenty of time for a softball game after dinner. Directly across from the store was a large field we designated the ball park. We had two bats and a ball, which was more tape than anything else, but no one seemed to mind. The playing field wasn't always available to kids my age because a group of boys several years our senior would sometimes commandeer the field, dig a hole several inches deep, and have a potato bake. We didn't see much sense in this. I suspect it was some kind of bonding thing.

On a typical evening, most kids started drifting home by 9:30 or 10 because it was getting too dark to see. Those who lingered would sometimes be involved in games of kick the can. Kids who went home listened to radios that broadcast big band music and "Your Hit Parade."

July Fourth was no typical day. Fireworks of all shapes and sizes were readily available from numerous stands, and we all agreed to spend $2 to ensure that the neighborhood would be banging and popping throughout the day. Although our parents briefed us on the potential hazards of lighting fireworks, we set them off from morning until night.

After dusk many gathered at the Excelsior Commons to watch the display sponsored by the town. We could see most of the high flying rockets from home, so this is where our family gathered to spend the final hours of that day.

Saturday nights were special too. Kids and many adults headed to the movies at the Excelsior Theatre, where admission cost a dime. The movies were two-reeler westerns, with a fifteen minute intermission while the operator changed reels on the projector. During intermission, the theatre manager conducted a drawing for plates and glasses. We hoped we wouldn't win, because it would entail an embarrassing trip onto the stage to collect the prize. Our hopes were never dashed.

We liked films starring Gene Autry and Roy Rogers, but especially enjoyed William Boyd as Hopalong Cassidy because he didn't waste time singing. Although an adult might give us a ride to the movie, we always chose to walk home so we could talk about what we had just seen. I saw my first color movie that summer, Errol Flynn and Olivia deHavilland in "Robin Hood."

A few weeks later another great film came to town, "The Wizard of Oz." We didn't realize that our children and grandchildren would still enjoy those two films more than sixty years later.

Most Eureka families had a car, and those who didn't walked. It was possible to walk to Excelsior and back on the road without seeing a car. Adults didn't hitchhike, but advertised their willingness to accept a ride by walking on the right side of the road rather than the left, and drivers almost always slowed down to offer walkers a lift. Kids didn't mind walking or riding bikes.

After the Fourth of July, we enjoyed the annual picnic at the Svithoid Home, a castle-like retirement residence with fishing boats and immaculately maintained three acres of ground. The event was supposed to be a fund raiser, and organizers sold tickets for five and ten cents, which attendees were supposed to exchange for refreshments. For several years, some young thief located where the rolls of tickets were stored and took enough to keep all his friends in food and drink throughout the day. I accepted these tickets unquestioningly, not wanting to look a gift horse in the mouth.

One of my more memorable and hair-raising experiences that summer came when I visited my friend Wally, who lived near Cook's Woods, which occupied 160 acres north of Wild Rose Lane and Eureka Lane. People had reported seeing mysterious lights in Cook's Woods, and while nobody went so far as to use the word "haunted," travelers sometimes took the long way to avoid passing the woods at night.

Wally's curiosity about Cook's Woods was more pragmatic than superstitious, so he invited me to bring along my flashlight and investigate the reported sightings. With no traffic noise, no street lights, and no moon, our trek into the woods that night felt ominous. After we had walked a quarter mile, I noticed large green eyes glaring from just beyond the illumination of our flashlights. Although I stopped in my tracks, Wally continued to forge ahead, oblivious of danger. After several other eyes appeared, Wally explained.

"I found these earlier this year. They're luminescent fungus that grow on trees in this part of the woods. Pretty neat, huh?"

Continuing deeper into the woods, Wally took me to an area that resembled a natural amphitheater with a marshy floor forty feet across and partially surrounded by steep hillsides that formed a bowl shape. Wally said he hoped the humidity and still air would help us see what he brought me there to observe.

After twenty minutes, we saw a faint glow that hovered a few feet from the ground. The illuminated ball drifted slowly toward one side of the hill and disappeared. Soon another ball about the size of a basketball appeared, then another and another. At one point, three balls were rising, hovering, drifting, and disappearing.

Marsh gas, generated by methane, was generated and became visible as balls of light. The show continued for a half hour and ended with one final ball that barely cleared the ground before disappearing. I never told anyone what I saw that night, but my fear of Cook's Woods was gone forever.

After two full months of summer adventures, things began to change. The end of the second week in August marked the beginning of dog days, the end of swimming season. Although hot, sultry days were upon us, signs of fall began to appear. The period between sundown and darkness shortened to the point where after-dinner activities were almost impossible, and new clothes and school supplies became the topics of conversation.

Friendships which had blossomed during the peak of summer now reverted to the fewer tried and true who lived closer to home. As the days grew shorter and the nights grew cooler, subconsciously we all accepted the upcoming inevitability--the end of the summer of 1939.

Robert Montrose, a retired polymer and mechanical engineer, lives in Plymouth. In 1999 he wrote about Eureka for the Excelsior Historical Society.

Ice Fishing With Dad
By Rebecca Braasch

One of my warmest memories of growing up in Minnesota is ice fishing. Forty years later, the taste of an egg salad sandwich, or the sight of a handcrafted minnow immediately transports me back to the snug little fish shanty on the lake- a welcome oasis in the dead of a cold winter.

Back then, in preparation for winter fishing, we handcrafted our own bait. A day or two ahead of time, Dad carved little fish shapes out of wood, hollowing out a space under the belly, into which molten lead was poured.

Although I wasn't allowed to handle or touch the lead, I remember being mesmerized by the fluidity of the steel gray liquid as it was being poured. It looked smooth, like milk. Dad explained that without the lead, the minnow would simply float, and fish just aren't interested in floating minnows. When the lead was cool, it was my job to paint the minnows, using colors to pique the curiosity of a big fish. Then Dad would add the finishing touch of fins, cut from tin.

The morning of our adventure, I wiggled with excitement while Dad gathered fishing poles, minnows and other paraphernalia. Mom packed a lunch of egg salad sandwiches, chips, pickles, apples and chocolate chip cookies, bundled me up, and sent us on our way with a hug and a kiss. Finally, we were ready to conquer those big bad fish-just me and my dad.

Reaching the frozen lake, I remember the eerie sound of ice cracking and groaning as we drove out across it to the fish house. Despite Dad's reassurances that the truck would not fall through, it still made me nervous. As children, trusting what adults tell us is often all we have to hold on to. This was one of those times, and Dad didn't let me down.

Arriving safely at our little house, Dad stoked a fire in the wood-burning stove. It didn't take long for the winter chill to give way to heat and the scent of burning wood. One corner of the fish house had a square-shaped hole where Dad would chip the ice out for fishing. While Dad chipped and scooped ice, I shed my hat, jacket, and snow pants and took my place in my chair next to the fishing hole.

When the hole was finally open and the chipped ice deposited outside, Dad floated the eggshells from the sandwiches that Mom had made for us down to the lake bottom. They helped reflect light from below, making it easier to see the fish as they swam into range. I remember how, when vehicles drove past outside, the water gently heaved up and down in the opening, threatening to flow over and onto the floor.

An intense little fisherwoman, I watched for fish as if I could simply will them to us. I leaned so far over the hole Dad had to tie a rope around my waist and attach it to the wall of the fish house to prevent me from falling in. Then finally, after a child's eternity, an unsuspecting fish would swim into range, curiously eyeing the primitive minnow dangling from Dad's fishing line. In a barely audible voice, I whispered, "Get him, Dad. Get him." Taking careful aim, he slowly raised his spear-on-a-rope, and in one swift, precise stroke, pierced the water, making his mark like a pro.

I recall the feelings of exhilaration as the skewered fish ascended through the ice hole, splashing my face in its frantic attempts to escape the end of Dad's spear - then the blinding of bright winter light bursting through the door as Dad pushed the fish off the spear with his boot outside. As a young lover of animals, I struggled with mixed feelings of triumph and regret as I listened to the sounds of the fish flopping around on the ice until it lay silent.

This scene repeated itself until we had enough fish, it got dark, or we got hungry again-- whichever came first. After making sure the fire in the stove was extinguished, we gathered up our catch and headed for home, anxious to tell Mom our fish stories.

Minnesotans still answer the call of the ice, but fish houses of today don't hold the old-fashioned charm of the one that lives in my senses. Today's ice shanties often house refrigerators, microwave ovens, televisions and beds. Heck, a person could just live out on the ice, and there are probably a few who do. But to me, nothing will ever compare to the heartwarming memories of the simple contentment of quality time spent fishing with Dad on the ice of Minnesota.

Rebecca Braasch lives in Brooklyn Park.

The Raven's Wing
by   Russell L. Christenson

In my work as a speech pathologist I often visit patients in their homes for therapy sessions. As much as possible, I like to conduct these sessions in the kitchen. Everyone seems more at ease when they're sitting at the kitchen table.

Occasionally, when I walk into that room I am greeted by a familiar aroma which immediately takes me back, in my mind, to my childhood on the farm. It is a blend of ingredients--the faint smell of wood smoke mixed with the smells of home-baked bread and home-rendered lard-- of pickling spices and pumpkin pie-- of sugar cookies and sugar-cured ham. It is a fragrance that permeates the very fabric of the room.

In about 1948 we moved to Minnesota to live with my grandparents, Carl and Mary Johnson. My parents had spent the years, during World War II in California, where my father had worked in the defense industries. Now they were going back to help my grandfather run the farm. I am not sure what time of the year we moved back, but my first (and most vivid) memories of Minnesota are of snow and very cold weather.

At that time, the farm had electricity but no running water. We had a refrigerator, but my grandmother cooked and baked with an old cast iron wood-fueled cook stove. The stove had four lids on the cooking surface.   These could be lifted up in order to build a fire under them. Above the cooking surface were two warming ovens, and on one side, was a reservoir which held several gallons of water.

While our food baked, the water warmed enough to provide hot water for washing dishes after the meal. In summer, the cook stove made the kitchen oppressively hot, and I would lose my appetite. However, in autumn and winter, I would come home from school to the welcome warmth and delicious smells of whatever Grandmother was cooking or baking.

The west end of the kitchen was taken up with cupboards, except for a window in the middle. A counter ran most of the length of the wall.

Under the counter were drawers for storing food, cooking utensils, and silverware. In the middle of this row of drawers was a large, metal-lined bin where grandmother kept her flour. In the flower bin she kept the raven's wing.

Grandmother would mix the ingredients for her bread and pastries on the counter top above the flour bin. Flour had to be sifted to eliminate lumps and ensure an even consistency. I always assumed that she used the raven's wing to dust the unused flour back into the bin, although I never saw Grandmother do that.

In summer, my mother and grandmother would can dozens of quarts of garden vegetables and fruits as they came into season. In August and September they would butter the flock of roosters we had raised all summer. Some of these would be boned and canned as well.

Late in the autumn, my father and grandfather would butcher a steer and a hog. Most of the meat would be taken to the locker plant for cold storage. However, the meat from the cow's flanks would be sewn into rolls, mixed with spices, and canned. This delicacy was known as rullepelsa.

The hog fat was rendered into lard and canned in quart jars. During the rendering process, bits of meat and pork rind would float to the surface of the rendering kettle. These were called cracklings, and the grown-ups thought they were delicious. I did not. The small of rendering lard was awful, but when all the work was done, the lard was in the jar, pure and white.

My mouth still waters when I think about the huge batches of popcorn we made in the winter. Popped in lard, then drizzled with pure creamery butter and sprinkled with real salt, it was a heart attack in a metal bowl.

By late autumn, much of the food we would eat during the winter was safely stored in quart jars in the basement. During winter, especially during the Christmas season, I would come home from school to find Grandmother busily baking bread or Scandinavian pastries. She might be making gudu, lefse, krumkakke, fatimon or rosettes. Whatever it was, she always stopped to give me a taste.

I think that it was after the winter of 1952 that Carl and Mary left the farm and moved to Owatonna. My parents bought the home place and farmed it until they retired. The old cook stove was hauled out into the woods and replaced by a modern electric range.

Not long ago I read that it was an old Norwegian custom to keep a raven's wing in the flour bin to ward off evil spirits. It must have worked because as far as I can remember, nothing but good ever came out of Mary Johnson's kitchen.

Russell Christianson is a speech pathologist and writer in Clinton, Missouri.

Country School in Nobles County
by Menno Dammer

Many remember the television series, "Little House on The Prairie," which was set in Walnut Grove. Every time I watched an episode that dealt with the country school, it brought back so many priceless memories.

Country School deserves a special place in this book, as does a special teacher who played such an important part in my life and the lives of so many other students who attended District 49 in the 1940's. Many country school teachers who taught in Minnesota in those days deserve recognition for what they accomplished through their students. Here is my story about how it all started in a one room country school house so many years ago.

There seems to be an attitude among today's younger set that walking a mile and a half to country school is a myth. During the years I conducted seminars with young captive audiences, the subject of attending country school came up often. Many would good-naturedly interrupt me and say, "Oh sure, we know how you walked to school in the snow," causing others to join in the ribbing. Although I tried my best to relieve their skepticism and convince them that the hardships we faced were real, I believe there were still many nonbelievers in the audience when I finished my pitch.

It all began when I was 5 years old in 1935, and my 7-year-old brother John took me by the hand as we walked that proverbial mile and a half down a gravel road to District 49, Grand Prairie Township, Nobles County, Minnesota. Kindergarten did not exist in those days, so I got an early start on my elementary education.

Although weather in southwestern Minnesota is mild in early September, I soon began to realize that no matter what the weather, my long morning walk would remain the same for the entire school year. With rare exceptions, I walked to school with my brother, rain or shine or snow. If we even had the nerve on a stormy day to ask our father for a ride to school, his usual answer was, "Walk-- it's good for you," and the subject was closed.

We adjusted to the climate by putting on an extra pair of bib overalls, overshoes, two jackets, heavy mittens, or a scarf wrapped tightly around our faces with only the eyes exposed. Even so, in severe weather, the eyebrows and eyelashes gathered such a coating of frost that it was hard to blink. As I watch my neighbors today drive their able-bodied teenagers three blocks to school in a luxury sport utility vehicle, I wonder if they could relate to going to country school.

The school day began with removing outer clothing in a porch area and hanging our jackets and caps in a row with all the others. If the weather was extremely cold, we kept our jackets on until the interior of that one large room was warm enough to enable us to write with fingers that were no longer stiff.

In one corner of the school house stood a very large coal furnace that often glowed red before the room was warm enough to allow us to remove our jackets. In case you might wonder who lit and stoked that furnace each morning, it was just another detail assigned to the one and only employee on the premises--the teacher. This responsibility required the teacher to arrive early on extremely cold mornings.

School began at 9 sharp. If students were outside, the teacher rang a large brass school bell and we responded immediately and filed in to our regularly assigned seats. The Pledge of Allegiance came next, and everyone had their turn leading the rest of the children in paying respect to our flag.

Education in a one-room school had a distinct advantage for younger students. They were able to absorb much of what was taught to students at a level of learning higher than their own because they were present during those class recitations. This constant repetition and review proved invaluable as years went by and the student moved up in grades.

Country schools no longer exist in Minnesota, but their memory lingers for those of us who had the opportunity to learn from the best. Today there are still many dedicated teachers who are overworked, underpaid, and under-appreciated for their efforts in teaching our children. Perhaps reaching back to a time when teachers were held in higher esteem may rekindle an interest in supporting those who prepare our young people every day for the best life to come.

Every morning our teacher or a student would read aloud from one of the classics for approximately fifteen minutes before regular school activities began. Readers included those in the first grade as they read from their primers. If any student had difficulty reading and another student giggled or showed any sign of ridicule, that student was severely punished - -and it never happened a second time. Every student who attended District 49 during the years that I was there turned out to be an excellent reader and public speaker whose accomplishments were reflected in their later high school grades

Recitation in country school was conducted in the following manner: Students in a particular grade were summoned to the front of the room, where the teacher asked questions from a previously assigned reading lesson. If any student missed more than two questions during the question and answer period, he or she was required to remain after school. The same reading assignment involved different questions by the teacher so every student, at every level, was motivated to study hard because they didn't relish staying after school.

Since I never had a classmate during my entire eight years of elementary school, my motivation to do well was obvious. There was no one to rely on to take up the slack when I didn't know the answer to a question! I had to do well because I was expected to come home after school to milk the cows while my father worked in the fields. There was no excuse for failing to know my lesson, either from the teacher's perspective, or my father's.

Teachers in those days were the best in their profession and showed a dedication that is hard to match. Although I was indoctrinated into the life of country school by another teacher in my earlier years, the best was yet to come. I soon realized that when Miss Arlene Heffele became our teacher as I began sixth grade in September of 1940

All the preparation that led up to getting yourself to country school in the morning would have meant little unless you had a teacher who was not only qualified to teach all eight grades of elementary school but who also maintained a dedicated effort throughout the year to gain the maximum from each student's potential. By my own calculations, she was only twenty-two years old at the time, but Miss Heffele exhibited wisdom beyond her years as she cultivated our ability to learn.

So much of what we learn in our formative years depends on how we are fed the information that is intended to remain with us for the rest of our lives. She gave everyone their respective reading assignments the day before recitation and expected each student to be prepared when class began. She asked pointed questions and expected direct answers. If you did not understand the question, she clarified it, and if you did not know the answer, she made sure you learned and understood it. No one was subjected to embarrassment in front of other students, and she allowed everyone to maintain their dignity throughout the recitation.

If you missed more than two questions during recitation, you were required to remain after school, when she would ask new questions from the original reading assignment. You did not know the questions in advance. Under her tutelage, you learned. She seldom assigned homework in addition to the reading assignment because she believed it was the teacher's responsibility to make sure that her students were learning properly, not the parents' responsibility.

Recess time in a country school usually meant playing games like softball on the school grounds, and the teacher was very much involved. Miss Heffele made sure we learned and understood good rules of sportsmanship and that we helped those who had less athletic ability than others. She emphasized teamwork and compassion in everything we did under her control.

She appeared to enjoy participating in sports as much as the students did, but when recess was over and everyone went back into the classroom, it was business as usual. When school was over, you did not leave until you were excused from the classroom. In the entire three years that she was my teacher, I never heard anyone utter an unkind word about Miss Heffele. I know she was proud of me when I graduated from the eighth grade, and she gave me the diploma that still hangs on the wall in my study-- almost sixty years later.

Miss Arlene Heffele, the teacher who prepared me for high school, college, and eventually my career, helped so many youngsters for life but

Miss Arlene Heffele poses with the students of District 49 in Nobles County. The author, a seventh grader, stands on the far right.

probably never realized how much she has done for all of us. When I had the opportunity to meet with her at Adrian's 125th celebration in June of 2001, it was an emotional moment for both of us. She was so pleased with our reunion and the credit I gave her for preparing me for life.

Today she resides with her husband Lee in a retirement home in Adrian, and she must have some wonderful memories of her own. She is a shining example of what made country school great.

Arlene Heffele Lais will always be special in my life, but I still call her "Miss Heffele" because to call her "Arlene" doesn't seem to show the respect she has always deserved. Teachers like her sacrifice so much and receive so little gratitude for their accomplishments. Thank you, Miss Heffele, and all the other school teachers who helped make us what we are today. We owe you so much!

Menno "Spike" Dammer served in the Navy, graduated from Pepperdine University, and earned a Masters' Degree in public administration from USC. Retired from the Los Angeles Police Department, he writes a weekly column for the Nobles County Review.

Farm Boys and Gophers
by Menno Dammer

Living on a farm in southwestern Minnesota meant having to deal with creatures of all kinds, especially gophers, the pests responsible for Minnesota being known as The Gopher State. Gophers were not considered friends to the farmer's corn crop, so measures that could be taken to reduce their population were necessary.

While my sister jumped rope with her girl friends, I did what most farm boys did on a Sunday afternoon, played baseball in the pasture or hunted gophers with my buddies. Besides this being a recreational activity, there was the potential of money to be made. Since thinning gopher population was too gruesome for the girls, it was traditionally accomplished by farm boys.

As an incentive for farm boys to do what they could to reduce the number of gophers, local townships offered a bounty. As near as I can recall, presenting two front paws of a gopher was worth two cents. It took quite a few paws to make a trip to town worthwhile, so young farm boys and their dogs had to do a lot of hunting.

If you had a good old dog, preferably two dogs, a long string of binder twine, a bucket and a nearby creek, you had the makings of what might turn out to be good gopher hunting. We farm boys considered this a good sport on a Sunday afternoon or any other time we didn't know what to do with our time.

The hunter began hunting by walking through the pasture that existed on everyone's farm. A shrill whistle often drew a gopher out of its hole to see what all the commotion was, so the hunter had to be alert and watch as the critters darted back into their holes. The dog would usually spot them first, run to the hole, and stand guard while the hunter went to the creek to fetch a bucket of water.

Sometimes an over-zealous dog would start digging so feverishly that he would plug the hole beyond repair. Most dogs were so used to hunting gophers that they just stood by while the hunter poured water into the hole, and placed a loop of twine around the hole as a snare. If only a small amount of water had been poured in the hole before it reached the top, it could only mean one thing. The gopher had already plugged the hole behind him to avoid drowning as he scurried down the hole. If you kept pouring water down the hole and it never filled to the top, it meant the gopher had his own release valve where the water was running out of another hole in the area. That's where the second dog would come in and look for a gopher coming out of another hole nearby.

The exchange between gopher and dog was something to behold because each was trying to outsmart the other. If the water quivered after the hunter poured a substantial amount down the hole, he knew the gopher was about to come to the surface to avoid drowning. At that precise moment the hunter had two choices. He would either let the dog grab the gopher as he showed his face, or pull on the twine and snare the gopher. I preferred the dog method because the dog was usually faster than I was when I closed the trap with a snare.

This sport was thoroughly enjoyed by farm dogs. Whenever you took a bucket with you and went out to the pasture, your dog knew instinctively that you were about to hunt gophers, his favorite sport too. Perhaps the reference to a dog as man's best friend originated with the attachment between farm boys and their dogs.

Hunting gophers was an important part of life on the farm for a boy in the old days. If you don't believe it-- just ask another old farm boy!

Taping for Emergencies
by Suzanne Nielsen

November of 1963 started out cold, with an enormous amount of snow. We were bored. We needed some adventure, some potential danger. We heard about Devil's Hill from older kids but hadn't yet experienced just what a great sledding hill it truly was. We were about to find out.

Brucie Roberts broke his leg going down Devil's Hill last winter. Robbie McKenna lost three toes on his left foot that same winter. I heard two stories. First, the toboggan ran over his foot, then the toes broke off because they were so cold. Then I heard that his boot fell off going down the hill; the boot with his toes left inside was never found.

That wouldn't happen to us because of the tape. We planned ahead.

"Tape over the hole," Sheryl told her sister Laurie when she discovered the exposed knee after pulling up her snow pants. "Either that, or stay home. Don't come if you're going to be a baby about being cold. We don't want to come back for a long time." Laurie knew she was outnumbered, and would get no sympathy out of us. She either had to tough it out or stay home. She was going to tough it out.

We each took turns taping our wrists with masking tape so no snow would get into our mittens and leave our wrists red with cold, then warm, as they set in for frost bite. I had taken the thick masking tape out of the utility drawer of our kitchen. I knew my Dad got it free from Chuck, the neighbor. He worked at 3M and got to bring home tape whenever he wanted. My parents didn't like me to use it, though. They felt better about having several rolls of the tape on hand, unused, just in case of an emergency. I'm not sure what was considered an emergency, but I knew using the tape was not okay, even under circumstances I considered an emergency-- potential frostbite.

My parents knew Sheryl and Laurie's dad also worked at 3M. They thought we should use their tape for our emergency. But Sheryl and Laurie only had the skinny masking tape at their house so I offered the thick, sturdier tape to keep us warmer and dryer.

After we taped up our wrists, we taped our ankles, just above the boot line and on down the boot. The plastic bags we wore over our socks, before putting on our boots, would help keep us drier and more comfortable. The tape would prevent us from losing a boot or mitten on the hill that we'd heard so many horrific stories about.

Off we went, the three of us, one of us always wanting to be in charge of the other two. I knew if I volunteered to go down the hill first, I would get my chance to be in charge. This was something any sledding expert wanted-- to go down first and to take charge.

This hill wasn't called Devil's Hill for nothing. After climbing the eight-foot fence and walking straight north for a good 45 minutes, we knew we had come upon the blood and guts of this adventure. Here was the hill we had only heard about until now. There was no mistaking it. It was the biggest and steepest hill I had ever seen in my 7-year life.

Laurie chickened out. She wasn't going to have anything to do with the hill. She started complaining about her taped knee. It was cold. We hated her whiny voice and decided to shove her face in the snow and threaten to push her down the hill if she didn't shut up. She surrendered to our threats.

Sheryl and I couldn't decide who was going first. Suddenly I didn't want to be the leader anymore, and told her I would let her go first because I had been in charge of the SLS club the last two times. SLS stood for Suzanne, Laurie and Sheryl, although Sheryl thought it stood for Sheryl, Laurie and Suzanne.

I told Sheryl that from now on, if she went down the hill first, at least until the spring thaw, it could be the Sheryl, Laurie, Suzanne club. It was too tempting an opportunity to pass up so there she was, getting situated on the four-person toboggan, ready to embark on an event that could change her life forever.

I must have been out of my mind. The SLS club would be under her dictatorship until spring. What was I thinking? I told her to get off the toboggan. I was going down. It was my toboggan, and I decided to take charge. Before I knew it, while I was still standing, the toboggan took off at a speed unfamiliar to me. We were flying down the hill. I struggled to bend down, while still remaining on the toboggan. Sheryl was screaming and I didn't want to know why. I didn't want to see what felt like the tunnel ride of my death. I just stared at the tape on my wrists and made my silent apologies to my parents for using the whole roll in an attempt to save ourselves from frostbite.

I was falling to my death, and I knew it. I was sorry, and I hated Laurie for knowing better. I wished I could have had a hole in my snow pants. I then would have had an excuse for not going down this hill, and I wouldn't be about to die from slamming into one of the huge oak trees that gave Devil's Hill its name in the sledding game.

We gradually stopped--not abruptly by a tree--not by bumping into lost boots with toes still intact, but just by coming to the end of the steepest hill I had ever seen this far north of the Rockies. I'd seen the Rockies in ski posters at Hoigaard's. Devil's Hill was much bigger than any of those. Devil's Hill was too big to talk about.

We made it alive--intact--but unable to tell a soul without getting grounded for sure. Our parents were bound to find out if we told a single person. We had to be nice to cry-baby Laurie, or she would tell.

That day we took on Devil's Mountain with a vengeance. We went down it standing up. We went down it standing up and yelling, "shit! " Laurie never went down the Mountain. She didn't care about the experience she'd never be able to talk about. It pleased her enough to know she kept her tape in good shape.

As a matter of fact, we were able to put all the tape back on the empty roll from Laurie's wrists and ankles. It wasn't as smooth looking as before its use, but it kept the household quiet for a while. We kept Laurie quiet by making the club every now and then the LSS club. Meaning, yes of course, she was in charge-- not earning that responsibility because of sledding guts, but for saving tape, in case of emergencies.

Suzanne Nielsen grew up in St. Paul's east side. A wife and mother, she loves to write fiction, essays, poetry, screenplays and memoir. She teaches writing at Metropolitan State University.

Tint
by Suzanne Nielsen

Ellen's house was a special place to visit, especially on Sunday evenings. She lived next door to Aunt Lil, whose house I went to whenever my Mother tired of me, which seemed all the time. Ellen was an older friend of mine. I think she was older than Aunt Lil, and Aunt Lil was the oldest person I knew. Aunt Lil didn't like Ellen much because she was Swedish. She told me that Swedes don't keep house and they are stingy.

Ellen's house belonged only to Ellen, and she shared her coconut and cocoa with me every Sunday evening--hardly what I would call stingy. Our Sunday evenings revolved around watching Walt Disney on her television, in living color. I would always arrive early so I could watch the peacock spread its wings, a different color for each feather spread. Ellen would fiddle around with some of the knobs and change the color a bit as the peacock became a rainbow of color, making it more green or red, what she called tint. She told me that the colorful peacock was supposed to be the boy peacock, that in nature things were that way. The males were beautiful, and the females were bland and more subdued.

She said that was only true of birds however, and I was much prettier than Kenny, who lived across the street. I asked her if I was prettier than my brother Lawrence because Aunt Lil liked him best, and I couldn't figure out why. She said of course I was, and I believed her because she never asked him to come over and watch Walt Disney in living color.

Each Sunday evening, a few minutes before 6, I would run out of Aunt Lil's back door and jump the fence, take three steps at a time, and like magic, I would enter Ellen's wonderful world of living color. I didn't care if Aunt Lil thought my quick way of getting to Ellen's un-lady-like because Ellen said it was just as important to be a kid as it was to be a lady. Ellen thought it was amazing how much speed I had in my stride and said she wished she was a kid instead of a lady. I thought she was both.

Ellen would always have hot cocoa on the stove and shredded coconut for us to eat. I got to use a plate with a turkey on it for my coconut so I wouldn't get it all over the floor. Ellen didn't have a dog, and she said she was just a particularly clean Swede.

I would dent the couch cushions with my body, making it comfortable, just for me. Ellen would watch and laugh until I got situated. Then she would tease me by asking me to go fetch some cocoa. I never knew she was teasing me, and there I'd go, running into the kitchen to retrieve Ellen's cup of hot, steamy cocoa. I'd sit back down, with my usual ritual of denting the cushions to my liking. Ellen would say, "You forgot the marshmallows." I'd be off and running like a kid, hurrying to get back because the living color peacock was about to appear.

Ellen was always grinning and I think giggling, because her whole body shook. Then she would wink with one eye at me. I knew this meant she liked me. Right then and there, she taught me how to wink like that with one eye. She said she learned how to wink when she was a kid, that kids and ladies alike could wink at one another if they felt like it. I winked at her from then on, during every station break of Walt Disney. I kept the winking a secret between Ellen and me. I never saw Aunt Lil wink, and I was sure she wouldn't think of it as lady-like. I wasn't sure I would like to give a wink to her anyway.

So there it was, the start of our event, Ellen's and mine. There was the peacock. There were the beautiful colors, and there was Ellen introducing me once again to this thing called tint. She must have been the richest woman in the world, for this television was bigger than our kitchen table-- or so it seemed. There was Tinkerbell, waving her wand, and with every blink of both my eyes, a new color firework would appear. This was the life-- sitting here with Ellen, eating coconut on turkey plates, sipping hot chocolate like ladies did their coffee, watching something so beautiful as living color.

When I'd return to Aunt Lil's, she'd ask what Ellen and I did. I lied every Sunday night to her about that. Sometimes I'd say we played Chinese checkers; sometimes I'd tell her we painted flowers on Ellen's doorknobs with tempera paints.

No matter what I told her we did, she didn't act surprised, which is the response I wanted, for if she knew that Ellen and I watched television for an hour, she'd never let me go back for more. She thought watching color television would ruin my eyes and make me unable to have babies-even if I sat far away.

I could go on and on about what Ellen and I did with Aunt Lil if need be, but there was never a need for me to give any more information. I'd go on and on in my head though, thinking how much fun it would be to paint those flowers on Ellen's door knobs, trying not to drip any paint on the floor, yet knowing that because she was a particularly clean and lady-like Swede, she'd wink at me first, then wipe up the drip.

The Farm Near Hastings
by Marilyn Mikulewicz Baranski

I feel that I touched the beginning of time---Minnesota time-- on the farm near Hastings where I lived as a child.

Seven years ago, my aunt and I visited that farm again. I had flown in from California, and we left our rental car on the gravel road outside the old driveway, as we feared we would get a nail in our tire. Our lovely dairy farm had been purchased in 1959 in a mass buyout of similar farms by the Iowa Development Company, which later went bankrupt and was bought out by a California company, which also went bankrupt or something. Anyway, they had rented out the farmland, and the pastures, and home sites had been left to die or revert to nature. No one had lived in any of those farms in close to forty years. I knew our huge old barn had burned on a Halloween night, and sadly, from what I had heard, the house was no longer standing either. The company had not wanted any of the buildings. They had planned to make their billions on land--just land.

I wanted a touch of my past--a couple of old bricks from the house, iris bulbs and a couple antique rose clippings from the Victorian style flower teardrop in front of the house, and maybe just something personal such as a left-behind toy or piece of molding or a doorknob--something that said I had been alive on that old farm. The want burned inside me.

My Aunt Martha and I strolled down the driveway commenting on box elder trees to our left and how the cedar tree windbreak my father planted was now massive and overgrown. Nature had reclaimed the land that the early Irish pioneers had made into a productive farmstead. The little driveway was surrounded by overgrown brush. In the center of the old yard, however, was a clear area probably used for tractor turn-arounds and bonfires for intruder parties. It had been a record breaking rain year, and a little mud puddle remained in the clearing. I could hear the bees, see the thick tree growth that had once been the lawn where I played. I could see foot prints of all God's creatures. We eyed human foot prints, deer prints, horse prints, large birds and tiny sparrow prints, rabbits, maybe fox or dog prints, and then my eyes centered on huge claw marks--perhaps about the size of four or even six of my hand prints.

"Bear!" my aunt whispered. She turned, and trotted up the driveway. I could barely keep up with her 83-year-old body as we hurried the quarter mile to the safety of the rental car.

We were about twenty-some miles south of St. Paul in an area where people had safely lived for well over a hundred years. Exactly how did bear get there? Not once had anyone ever mentioned bear in all the years of my existence. Did they ride in on a log from northern Minnesota, or had they been hiding out all those years? Who knows! The one thing that I did know was that no souvenir was worth becoming a bear burger or whatever snack bears like.

As I plan to stay frightened of animals that might eat me, all I have are memories of the home that formed who I am. Nothing big ever happened there, but I am drawn to recall the life I lived in that house. My life probably was not dissimilar to those of the first settlers who survived on early Minnesota farms, and from those experiences I feel I have touched history. Perhaps others will find events of their pasts as I remember my first home.

I remember the big old brick house, sort of a farm house Gothic. I remember sitting on the floor in the blue living room with its cabbage rose drapes on a particularly windy night when the colored leaded glass portion up above the bay window smashed across the floor. I loved that leaded glass window, but due to economics and the style of the time, it had to be replaced with plain window glass. I remember the bulls eye moldings above the doors and windows. I remember years later walking into a house in San Francisco with the same molding and feeling a sense of home and a need to protect the house. To me, old houses take on a sense of their own being, personification. My love for them, I know, comes from having spent the first years of my life in our gem.

The house had started its life as a smaller home up near the highway--Highway 55- between Hastings and Rosemount, but then it was moved by horses a half mile back to the center of the farm. My research at the Dakota County Historical Society told me that in perhaps 1830 to 1840, the house rested on blocks for a few years just above a small old rock quarry used to build the foundations of all of the farm's buildings.

Horses brought it up out of the pasture to higher ground, where it was greatly expanded. It had additions of a brick sheathing and fancy molding and a curving staircase with some very wide triangular steps, perfect for setting up a dollhouse. It was not unlike the picture of houses shown in *Early American Life*. There was a heavy planked porch in the back and a huge glassed-in cement porch in the front, which had a cistern underneath. My mother always kept a heavy table over the cistern area so none of us kids could open it and fall in.

The rooms were only seven feet high, which is pretty consistent with the early American houses in the East. My parents greatly remodeled the house-- putting in a new kitchen with birch cabinets, a new bath, upgraded insulation and a new heating system. Fortunately, they left the old wainscoting and the wonderful nooks that our next brand new house with its sleek, boxy rooms never had. For a long time I dreamed of buying the building area back and filling the old house with my old press back chairs, my pump organ, and the farm furniture I have brought out of Minnesota piece by piece.

That house is a tie with the very first settlers who homesteaded the land along the river. You could find arrowheads all over the pastures. Just above Spring Lake, the land was gorgeous and park-like. The top part, near the highway, had flat, heavy soil suitable for growing corn and alfalfa, while the bottom area had sandier soil. It was probably an old river bottom thousands of years ago. The center, the pastures, had rolling hills which were covered with gooseberry bushes and big old oak trees. The cows kept it mowed, which made it a perfect place for kids to play-- if they watched where they stepped. Today the lower area is being made into a state park or recreational area.

I can close my eyes and touch those early immigrants who first walked on the land, felled the trees, and built the buildings. Some of those early settlers seemed to like liquor. I remember finding very old whiskey bottles along the fence lines, which might explain why not all of the fences are any too straight. I remember the huge old barn that was about one hundred twenty feet long with high haymows and lightening rods on the roof.

I remember the pet calves--all named Blackie. I braided lovely clover necklaces for them, and a minute after I slipped them over their heads, they ate my hard work. I remember pet banty chickens I had every summer. I would build them ladders to go into the elm tree. Don't ask. One little rooster hid behind the gas tank and attacked my legs each afternoon as I came home from school. We soon ate an unusually small chicken for dinner.

A previous owner, Tom Rowe, hanged himself in that old barn during the Depression, leaving a wife and three daughters to manage on their own. What was he thinking?

I remember long machine sheds with tin roofs that made a lot of noise when it rained, and the gypsies who came along and tried to sell a silver paint job for the roof. Fortunately we had read the Dakota County Tribune so, unlike others, we weren't fooled! And there were chicken houses and pig houses and corn cribs and the silo that came down in a wind storm and was soon replaced by a new silo costing $425. I remember lightning storms that lit up the yard at night.

I remember that our telephone ring was two shorts and a long, and how we all listened for that ring. My mother, however, was one of the folks who would secretly listen to other conversations. My mother also listened to this big old radio, and one day when Stella Dallas was suffering through a heart wrenching adventure, the radio disappeared in a cloud of gray smoke. Shortly after that we had a television. I was about 6, and the first night we all stayed up late in wonderment to watch the news. Some guy had escaped from prison, and his picture was flashed on the screen. I was sure that convict was looking right out of the TV screen and through me.

I remember waking up one morning to hear my mother tell that she had gone to my baby brother in the middle of the night while my father slept on in their bed. We had had company until about 10, and my tired mother had left dishes and coffee cups on the kitchen table. After going to bed, she heard people in the kitchen in the middle of the night.

She heard chairs moving, dishes rattling, and drawers opening. She heard voices of several people--men and women. She was afraid to yell for my father, who might be killed going downstairs to investigate, afraid the baby would cry, and afraid the intruders would come upstairs.

She planned to drop the green heavy jardiniere on their heads if they came up the stairs. She stayed awake, not moving until dawn. And that was it. The intruders never came back, and we never knew any more about the them, but that was the night we started to lock the front door.

I remember hating to work in the garden. We grew everything and everything needed weeding. Except for Sundays, shoes never touched my feet all summer. My mother wore shoes, as she was an adult, but somehow she managed to sunburn the bottoms of her feet picking strawberries. I wasn't too fond of canning either, but I surely did a lot of it.

I was enamored of rearranging the cellar where all the canning jars were kept. The cellar was a deep room under the kitchen lined with shelves and big rock matching the quarry area in the pasture. I rearranged the jellies, string beans, pickles, corn, tomato sauce, soup mixes, pickles, canned chicken, pears and peaches, applesauce, sauerkraut, relishes and so on and so on until the jars were perfectly color coordinated. I remember, too, there were bushels of potatoes and carrots that would stay fresh in sand until about April. The smell was wonderful as we always went to Wisconsin to buy fragrant sweet apples to store in the cellar.

It was the kind of work no kid likes, but during the years I taught US History, I could tell the kids things the book only hinted about. California kids, or at least my California kids, haven't a clue that you can actually put a piece of potato with an eye in the ground and grow more potatoes. I have told them all about growing crops, making sausage, bulk tanks for milk, corn pickers, hay bailers, canning, baby calves and even that chickens don't lay eggs a dozen in one sitting. We have made butter, homemade soap, candles, and even grew corn in a huge pail in the corner of the classroom near the window. All of this has given them a clue as to how our country was formed.

I feel a closeness with the early settlers who lived there a hundred years before. I imagine they too heard the rain on the roof and hated to work in the garden. I wonder if the women were strong and if the babies survived. Did they have picnics on the back porch, and did they love the smell of purple lilacs as much as I did? I wonder if they ever saw bear!

I still yearn for something to hold or something to love from that old farm. Just one snip of those wonderful antique roses in the front tear drop would look so great growing in our own rose garden today in California. What pure magic they performed when they appeared each Spring! I wonder which of the early settlers had the gentle heart to appreciate those roses. Someday I will go back and find my treasures-- provided the bear stay away.   Until then I have my memories

I was about 4 here-- on the farm near Hastings.

Marilyn Mikulewicz Baranski graduated from Rosemount High School and earned BS and MS degrees at Winona State University. She teaches in Vallejo, California, writes freelance articles, and collects antiques. She and her husband Fred have one adult daughter, Alicia Michelle.

Funeral Flower Girls in International Falls
by Madonna Hazen Erkenbrack

The ringing telephone awakened me. Should I grab a robe and go downstairs to answer it?

Saved by my father's voice. His side of the conversation went something like this: "Yes, I understand. They will both be dressed in their Sunday dresses, ready, and waiting for the black sedan to pick them up early Friday morning."

My sister was 5 years old and I was 7. We were seated immediately behind the mourners at the church. There was no remuneration for being a flower girl; it was considered to be an honor. Our names would be included in the newspaper article about the funeral.

As people approached the casket sobbing quietly or loudly, we flower girls began to sob along with the mourners. Our tears fell against the flower bouquets we were holding. Although we did not know the deceased, we expressed our sadness at his passing, and our tears undoubtedly triggered more tears among the mourners.

Just before the services, the funeral director whisked us out of the church and on to the cemetery. We usually stood on the loose dirt by the grave, still holding our flowers.

We were never asked to partake of refreshments or to socialize with grieving families. When we came home, we cleaned our shoes for Sunday school or for another funeral--whichever came first.

I have asked people--even funeral directors from various other places, but they have never heard of flower girls at a funeral. To the best of my knowledge, the custom was carried on in International Falls until fairly recently. Rather than small girls, they used a small boy dressed in a tuxedo-- like a ring-bearer at a formal wedding.

Young Oliver Twist wore a tall hat and walked behind hearses in Dickens' classic novel so maybe child mourners came from an English custom. An article about the death of Queen Victoria in 1901 mentions flower girls who were furnished with rags of crepe. Articles compiled by genealogists name funeral flower girls in Tennessee, Kentucky and Illinois as recently as the 50's and 60's. Since the practice was somewhat widespread, it seems strange that few people have heard of it.

It did not matter what your ethnicity or background or religion, the flower girl custom was followed in our town. My mother was New England English, and my father was Dutch. My early experiences as a funeral flower girl had a profound effect on me. It was not until years after I was married that I was able to attend a funeral without sobbing.

The author lives with her husband in California. She taught in Bricelyn and Austin, and taught secretarial studies at Macalester College in St. Paul. She enjoys bridge and travel.

Yearning
By Joyce Kennedy

When I was 7 and in second grade, I lived in a place in northeastern North Dakota called, quite simply, Grey. Not a town or a village, Grey was a consolidated school attended by farm children from many miles around it.

It was not the traditional, pristine, white one-room schoolhouse that dotted the plains at that time; instead, it was a four-room building. I was in the room for first, second, third and fourth graders. My father was the principal, the overseer of all the rooms, which included one for high school students.

My mother took care of what was called the teacherage, a white rectangular box of a house a few hundred feet from the school. Our family lived on the ground floor, and rented one of the rooms to Miss Zelpha Irvin, my teacher. Another teacher and his family lived on the second floor.

The two buildings, school and house, declared themselves on a landscape that stretched flat for as far as the eye could see. Some playground equipment sat in front of the school--an old, rusty swing set and a splintery wooden teeter-totter.

There was a playing field behind the school, and on one side, to the west, a row of scraggly trees that had been planted as a windbreaker. Bent and deformed, they were trees that had clearly given up on growing up.

I sit with my Shirley Temple doll, my dad Erling Logeland, and my sister Marlene on the steps of the teacherage.

Zelpha Irvin, on the other hand, had certainly grown up, and I thought she was the prettiest thing I had ever seen. She had brown curly hair and huge brown eyes with curly eyelashes. Her first name, to my mind, was fitting to her beauty. This was her first year of teaching, so she couldn't have been more than nineteen or twenty. In those days, young women attended normal school after high school for a couple of years of teacher training.

I learned a lot in Miss Irvin's room, partly because I had time to listen to the lessons for the third and fourth graders. To my delight, I learned about the parts of speech. What fun--like doing a puzzle! I learned about geography, too. It was amazing to think about other spots in the world besides North Dakota and Iowa, my two main references for place. More important, with Miss Irvin's help, I began to develop my lifelong love of reading.

Here is how it happened: One week, Miss Irvin started to read *Heidi* to the class, a chapter a day, each day, right after lunch. I was entranced. On Friday, after chapter five, I approached her shyly.

"May I borrow *Heidi* for the weekend?" I asked.

Sensing my need and with only a flicker of hesitation crossing her face, she replied, "Of course."

That weekend, Zelpha Irvin's parents came to drive her home to Langdon, as they did every weekend. She waited in the enclosed front porch for her parents, her big brown eyes looking out of the windows with impatience and yes, yearning. "Homesick," my parents said to each other.

Miss Irvin went off with her mother and father, and I had the magical book all to myself. I spent the whole two days propped up against the rusty swing set, coming into the house only when my mother insisted, to eat and sleep. It was early November, bleak and barren. Russian thistles--great, round, brown, prickly balls--came bouncing across the prairie, blown along by the ceaseless wind. They would skip across the playground, finally getting caught by the house, where they piled up to make a spiky webbed covering on its side.

I paid them no mind because I was in the Alps with Heidi and Peter and Grandfather. I was in the Alpine meadows tending the goats with Peter. I was picking flowers in the golden light of the sun. I was drinking goat's milk and eating Grandfather's cheese. I was sleeping in the sweet-smelling hay of the loft in Grandfather's mountain home. The mountains stretched up and up, sculptured against a sparkling blue sky. There were trees, thousands of trees--deep, dark, silent forests of trees that fringed the golden meadows.

I lived in the book for two days, discovering the rapture of reading. When the weekend was over and I returned to Grey, the landscape of my imagination included mountains, forests and fresh running streams. And I began to yearn.

It was then that my Norwegian grandmother added to that landscape and that yearning. Although she lived for most of the year in Bemidji with her daughter Dagny, she visited her sons and their families occasionally for six-week stints.

When she visited us, she and I shared a bedroom and a nightly routine. First, I would watch her brush her long gray hair, unbound, for one hundred strokes, something she assured me was a very good thing to do. She taught me the 23rd Psalm, and we would recite it together every night after we went to bed. The words, " Yea, though I walk through the valley of the shadow of death, I will fear no evil," always thrilled me-- another landscape to stir the imagination. Then, as we gently lulled into sleep, she would tell me stories of her girlhood in Norway.

Oh, but Norway was a beautiful place! The mountains, the fjords, the valleys, the trees! She told me that she went up into pastures in the summer and skied downhill to school in the winter. Could anyone have had a more idyllic childhood?

Truth is, North Dakota did not fit into my grandmother's landscape aesthetic. She did not think highly of treelessness and prairie. Bemidji was acceptable because it had lakes and pine trees. My parents used to kid that as soon as Grandma crossed over the state line to Minnesota, she thought she was in a better place, more comparable to Norway. She had me convinced, if not my parents.

I eventually crossed over to Minnesota, too, to live most of my life here, a place that satisfies my taste for gentle contours, lakes, green, forests of trees. Any yearning now goes in the other direction, back toward North Dakota with its enormous stretches of prairie, huge sky, waving grasses, wild roses growing along roadsides, its sweet smell of spring after winter thaw. It is etched deep inside my nervous system, as one's first lived-in landscape always is, for any person.

Joyce Kennedy was a teacher and administrator in Bloomington before retiring. Now she is a practicing poet and an enthusiastic gardener and grandparent with her husband, Wally Kennedy.

Growing up on the Range
by Virginia Anderson Trethewey

I was born in Minneapolis but moved with my parents and three siblings to the Iron Range, where I spent my childhood in Gilbert. After all these years, I still look back on those days with fondness.

My dad was a painter for the Oliver Iron Mining Company, a subsidiary of U.S. Steel. We lived in a company house, one of many that the company built for its employees. It had six rooms, and we paid $8 a month rent. At first we had an outhouse, but in the 20's the company installed indoor plumbing. What a luxury it was not to have to go outside in the cold or bathe in a galvanized tub in the kitchen Saturday night!

Every year the company awarded prizes to tenants who kept the nicest yards. This competition provided everyone with an incentive to keep their houses and property in top shape. Just below the company houses we had a park, which was actually an abandoned mining pit. Pin cherries grew from the walls of the pit, and there were also choke cherries, raspberries and wild flowers that we were allowed to pick. Part of that area included an abandoned water pit with concrete blocks left over from buildings. We kids used to play there, skipping from one block to another. It scares me to think how easily we could have fallen into the dirty red water between the foundation blocks. In winter when the water froze, we skated there.

Company working families were a mix of Slavs, Italians, Finns, Poles, and English with a sprinkling of Scandinavians. English were called Cousin Jacks, a term that originated from a time when labor was in short supply in the mines. Supposedly a typical remark made by English miners was that they had a cousin Jack back in England who was soon coming over to work.

The Range was known for its excellent schools, made possible by mining company taxes. Kids from Alcore, McKinley, Genoa and Sparta came to Gilbert for high school, and they got a good education. We learned foreign languages, had nice libraries, a swimming pool, teams, organizations, honor society, a Glee Club and other activities. Many of our graduates did well when they went on to college and other training.

Life in Gilbert during the 20's was happy and prosperous.   I remember skipping along the wooden sidewalks looking in every crack for a penny or a nickel. Children played outside and walked to Ely Lake for picnics and recreation. We were always intrigued by the knife sharpening man who would scout the neighborhood playing a music box trying to attract customers. Hearing his music, housewives brought their knives and scissors out to be sharpened.

On the Fourth of July, we had a big all-day party. Kids wore costumes and competed for prizes. We spent most of the day on Main Street participating in various games like the three-legged race. My mother made food ahead of time, and we had a case of cream soda in the basement. We'd run home to snack and return to Main Street for festivities that included a parade and fireworks.

My dad enjoyed the prosperity of the 20's. With money from the sale of his Minneapolis house, he bought a Maxwell with tan canvas covers on its windows. Although we were the envy of our friends as we rode along in this sporty car, my remembrances are not all positive. My dad chewed tobacco, and as he drove along he'd spit the juice out his window. The wind sometimes carried that juice right back into the back window, where I sat with my siblings.

Besides the Maxwell, we enjoyed other luxuries. Dad bought an Edison phonograph for $175, a nice big piece of furniture that made a beautiful addition to our living room. We listened to Enrico Caruso and Madam Schuman-Heink, two famous opera stars, and to popular music of the 20's. We bought a piano, and I took lessons. Music was an important part of our lives.

But the jubilant music of the Roaring 20's gave way to the plaintive strains of " Brother Can You Spare a Dime?" after the crash of 1929. During the Great Depression, the Oliver Mining Company scaled back production. When the complete mining location in Gilbert shut down, the company gave tenants the opportunity to buy their houses for $300. Some bought houses and moved them to Evelyth or Virginia, where plants continued to operate at low capacity. My Dad could not get a loan to buy our house, so we packed up and moved to Virginia in 1937.

As a painter and maintenance worker, my dad was able to work nine days a month at the Virginia facility. He was lucky; most miners had no work at all. I remember seeing idle miners whiling away the hours playing Chinese Checkers. Some people made and sold rag rugs. Everyone had a big garden, which helped feed their families. Occasionally the company nurse delivered a free bag of groceries, and this was greatly appreciated.

My brother got a job working for the Civilian Conservation Corps, one of President Roosevelt's social programs designed to put people back to work. He earned $30 a month plus board and room for two years, sent home all but $5 spending money, and still had enough to go to college.

I tried nursing school for a while and then got a job in a defense plant during the war. After a while I moved back home, and finally, in 1943, moved with my husband to Minneapolis.

After all these years, I still look back fondly at childhood days on the range. We used our imaginations to create fun and busied ourselves by enjoying life's simple pleasures. Surviving the Depression was no big deal because everyone was in the same boat. However, we came away from those hard times with an appreciation for the value of a dollar, and I have never been able to rid myself of my Depression mentality. After all these years, I still think twice before spending money.

A retired clerical worker, Virginia has lived in Robbinsdale for 52 years. Besides being a political activist and charter member of Women Against Military Madness, she enjoys reading and writing.

Parable of the Robbinsdale Robins
by Winifred Kaercher

Fifty-two years ago, when we purchased our home, the builder included a maple sapling as part of the landscaping. We considered this a family tree, and it grew over the years with our children. It was a wonderful tree with multi-trunks, perfect for climbing.

During the 60's, a pair of robins returned every spring to nest in their favorite spot in the tree. One year we had just had new carpeting installed, so when the robins appeared, my husband decided to give them a treat--a handful of carpet clippings. What a windfall! They got so excited that they spent the day weaving a nest with those ravelings.

The next day we looked outside, and there truly had been a windfall. There lay the nest on the driveway. What did Mr. and Mrs. Robin do? They promptly proceeded to rebuild their nest. I spent the day observing them from the flat roof as they took each carpet string to rebuild the nest. Then they would swoop over the house and go down to the lake two blocks away to fetch mud to cement their nest together. After several hours, their new home was complete--securely anchored in the tree this time. They raised their family, returned South for the winter, and returned the following spring.

By 1990, when our family tree had grown to mammoth proportions--forming an umbrella for the front yard with huge boughs resting on our roof, it seemed wise to cut it down and replace it with a new tree that was only seven and a half feet when we put it in. I told the nurseryman, " I don't have time to wait," and he gave me a fast-growing maple that has flourished.

Each spring this tree is a source of joy as the delicate tinge of green unfurls, providing shade and shelter for the bird choirs that serenade me. When that magic day in autumn arrives signaling change, lovely green transforms into a glorious crown of crimson foliage which blesses all who behold. What wonderful lessons we learn from God's creation!

Winifred Kaerchner lives in Robbinsdale and is a grandmother and a member of the Humane Society.

Some Minor Events of the 20th Century
by Albert W. Eaton

I was born in Bowbells, North Dakota, on October 13, 1908, but I lived most of the 20th century in various towns in North Dakota, Iowa and Minnesota. Not too many people can give a first-hand account of transportation by horse and wagon or tell you what they did during both World War I and World War II, but I can. When I was a kid, we didn't have electricity, a telephone, indoor plumbing or a car. I was 4 years old when the Titanic sank. The Wright brothers made their historic flight at Kitty Hawk just five years before I was born, so that gives you an idea of the progress I've seen and how times have changed since I was a kid.

I was the oldest of three children born to Clara Troska Eaton and Elmer Wells Eaton. Dad was in the grain elevator business, and we moved around a lot. By the time I graduated from high school in Madison Lake, I had lived in eight different towns. When a person moves to a new town, everything makes an impression on him because nothing is routine. Some of the things I remember most vividly, therefore, are the impressions and events that didn't make national headlines.

Dad got a job in Lismore the summer of 1920, so we moved from Cresco, Iowa. Dad was already working in Lismore, but our furniture had to be shipped by rail, which took time. The rest of the family spent time with Uncle Leon, who lived on a farm five miles north of North Mankato. While there I helped with chores and learned to milk a cow.

When our furniture got to Lismore, we moved into small living quarters connected to the Farmers' Elevator where Dad worked, and which were included as part of his wages. In that house we were very close to the elevator operations, and one day a freight car pulled in close to the elevator with its door open.

Among the things in the boxcar was an open pail of candy. I don't know how it happened to be open, but Mom, my sister and I took advantage of a rare opportunity, hoisted ourselves up to the boxcar, and helped ourselves. My sister and I jumped out of the car when the train started switching cars and the candy car started moving. Still inside, however, was my mom. She was pretty embarrassed when she realized the railroad men were watching her, but she managed to hop out.

We stayed in that house only a short time because we needed more room. Dad had written us when we were at Uncle Leon's house that he had bought a farm. When we arrived, however, I was disappointed to see that it was only a house with a couple of acres. It was a big job to clean the house because it had been left in quite a mess.

The walls had hundreds of nail holes we had to fill, and the place was infested with bedbugs. We had to put gasoline between the wall and the mop board in an effort to exterminate them. My friend Harold Von Rosen and I rode our bicycles to Adrian to buy sulfur candles to burn to kill the bugs. When we finally got the house fixed up, it was very nice. It had a cistern but no indoor bathroom.

I was in sixth grade in Lismore at St. Anthony's Catholic School, and I served as an altar boy. We had Notre Dame nuns, and one of them said she knew all about me because she had talked to the sisters from Cresco. I must have had quite a reputation.

On the east side of Lismore was a creek, and the railroad had dug deep enough to make a small lake, which is where they got water for steam engines. Trains would stop on the bridge and pump water into their boilers. The water was deep enough to go over our heads, and that is where I learned to swim.

The railroad that ran through town was a branch line from Worthington that had a freight train with one car on the end for mail and passengers. One day it was reported that an outlaw was running loose and might be on that day's train. Two armed men created excitement when they met the train and searched it, but they found nothing.

Dad bought his first car while we lived in Lismore, a second-hand Ford Touring Car for $200. The top could be put back in nice weather, and in winter we could put on side curtains. Having a car gave us the opportunity to visit friends we had left behind in other towns. But along with our new freedom came an added responsibility. Dad bought a cow, and it became my responsibility to look after her and milk her.

Because of problems with the elevator, we didn't stay long in Lismore. In the fall, we moved to the nearby town of Iona. Because we hadn't yet made the move when school started, my sister and I stayed at the Anderson Rooming House, though we were only in seventh and sixth grades at St. Columbo School. Dad would pick us up and take us back to Lismore every Friday and deliver us back to Iona on Monday morning.

I was an altar boy again, and one day Father Dolly came to school and told everyone how nice and loud I said the prayers at mass and how all the other boys should do the same. Proud to be the best, I continued to speak louder and louder until one day Father turned around during mass and told me to pipe down.

Father Dolly had a business interest in the local movie house, and he would give us movie tickets if we served mass. This proved to be an encouragement to my religious fervor. The first and only time I fainted was while serving mass. After bowing down while kneeling to say a prayer, I continued to stay in that position until I rolled down the altar steps. My sister accused me of falling asleep, but I still maintain that I fainted. However, her assessment of my bad behavior might have been justified.

When our first report cards came out, I came home with a zero in deportment. Gosh, I must have been a holy terror to receive a zero! Dad took me out to the wood shed for a spanking. I yelled quite a lot but didn't get hurt. After that he took me to the convent and made me apologize to the sisters. On my next report card, my deportment mark was one hundred.

In the spring, our baby sister was born and we needed more space. We moved about a block and a half to a bigger house, where we had a telephone but no bathroom.

We had stored a bookcase and some books in a building behind the elevator, but when we brought them to the new house, we discovered about thirty books missing. We put an ad in the paper saying we knew who had stolen the books and if they were not returned, we were prepared to take action. The next morning about half the books sat on our doorstep, but we never saw the rest of them. Either two people were involved, or the one person was only half honest.

Taking care of the cow kept me pretty busy. I staked her in the vacant lot next to our house. I also raised chickens for 4-H and won a couple of blue ribbons at the county fair in Slayton.

When I wasn't taking care of livestock, I liked to play in the big pasture with a creek on the edge of town. This was a perfect place to pretend I was a camper. I took wood, matches and a potato, and I built a fire and cooked lunch. I always dreamed of being someone else.

When I grew tired of camper dreams, I turned my attention to becoming a wrestler. My friend Melvin Koob, who was two years older, wanted to take a correspondence course in wrestling from Farmer Burns. The cost of the course ranged from nine to thirty-five dollars, depending on how good a wrestler you wanted to become from having taken a correspondence course. We decided to take the nine dollar course and sent Farmer Burns a dollar each month. I guess that old saying, "You get what you pay for," applies here. We didn't pay much, and we didn't get much.

There were many things to entertain us in those days. One time a tent show pitched their tents in the lot next to our house and put on a production of *Uncle Tom's Cabin*. I can recall attending card parties, amateur theatrics and get-togethers at friends' houses. We had a pool hall and a bowling alley. When I graduated from eighth grade, my aunt gave me a tennis racquet. I was so thrilled that I slept with it.

In 1923 we moved to Hadley, about twelve miles from Iona. Every night we loaded small things into the car and carried as much as we could to the new house, which was owned by the elevator. The night before our final move, I stayed with friends. The next morning I got up early and walked the cow to Hadley. Everyone thought it would take us all day, but the cow and I confounded the skeptics and made the trip in a half day.

My sister stayed in Iona to finish eighth grade and roomed with a family, and I had to go in to Slayton for high school. I walked over to the grocery store and hitched a ride with another family. A few times when the weather was bad, we took the train to high school. Occasionally a farmer picked us up with a team and sled when the weather was bad.

During the summer of 1924, I worked on a farm. One of my jobs was to herd cows on horseback. This gave me a chance to be a cowboy. My boss's brother was a carnival wrestler, and Dad took me to Slayton to watch him wrestle once.

The New York Yankees' pitcher George Pipgrass came home after the World Series and pitched a game for Hadley against Lismore at the Slayton Fairgrounds. It was a cold day, and Lismore won a huge upset. Sports analysts blamed the weather. We went to see a traveling girls' baseball team play at the fairgrounds, and we watched a silent movie, *Covered Wagon*, while the Slayton band played the background music.

Dad bought a new Chevrolet four-door sedan with a self-starter, and we drove to Sioux Falls to attend a piano concert by Paderewski. A medicine show came to town and performed every night for a week. The last night they showed *Birth of a Nation*, the first twelve-reel movie made.

We had lots of picnics and took trips to Worthington, Tippcota, and Lake Shetek. Lake Shetek had a an island called Walhalla a short distance from shore, and on that island was a dance hall, picnic grounds, and a baseball diamond. One end of the dance hall was mirrored. Tippcota had an octagonal dance hall with a bandstand in the middle.

My cousin Edward came to visit, and I taught him to swim. We would put on our suits and walk across town, which some townsfolk considered indecent. The lake was so shallow we would walk and swim across it and back again. Those who didn't know how shallow the lake was thought I was a terrific swimmer.

In the spring of 1926, a salesman came to Hadley to meet with the elevator board members to sell the idea of installing a feed mill and combining it with the elevator. Hadley decided against the idea, but I think this is where Dad got the idea to go into business for himself.

He found a building that he could convert into a feed mill for $1200 in Madison Lake, so the Eaton family moved again. Movers from Mankato slept in the truck, and the next morning loaded everything but the cow. My sister and I stayed with friends and finished the school year in Slayton before moving with our parents to Madison Lake in June.

I don't suppose these remembrances are as earth-shattering as the major historical events I lived through, but they do show how times were different and how, in spite of our lack of modern conveniences, we rolled with the punches and made it all work.

Dad bought his first car while we lived in Lismore, a second-hand Ford Touring Car for $200. The top could be put back in nice weather, and in winter we could put on side curtains. Having a car gave us the opportunity to visit friends we had left behind in other towns.

Albert Eaton taught high school social studies and music from 1937 until 1974. During that time he worked in Hardy and Creighton, Nebraska, and in Fulda, Le Center and Bloomington, Minnesota. He and his wife Esther live in Bloomington and have two adult daughters.

Jesse James Probably Had a Good Laugh
by Wayne Eddy

I'm a member of the James-Younger Gang. Every year when Northfield celebrates The Defeat of Jesse James Days, we perform historically accurate dramatic raid re-enactments of the time in 1876 when Jesse James, Frank James, Cole and Jim Younger and their gang tried to rob the First National Bank. The gang robbed banks, stagecoaches, and trains for years and killed about twenty people before they got to Northfield. In 2001, we celebrated the 125th anniversary of their historical defeat.

Joseph Lee Haywood, the cashier at the bank, was the treasurer of Carleton college and a member of the city council. He was acting cashier for the bank because the president of the bank was in Philadelphia for the United States Centennial. Heywood would not give up the money, even though Jesse threatened to slash his throat. He said the vault was on a time lock, but in reality it wasn't. Frank shot him in the head, and then citizens sprang into action.

Northfield takes pride in the fact that townsfolk thwarted the gang. Citizens took matters into their own hands and ambushed gang members from the upper story of the hotel and from the hardware store. Although Frank and Jesse James got away, two of their gang died in the street. Cole Younger and his brother Jim were captured and sent to Stillwater Prison.

When we do our re-enactments several times each September, we draw crowds of several thousand people. And we try to recreate the scene exactly as the raid happened, according to our historical research. The horses and costumes are real and we follow the same sequence of events that occurred on that famous day, but the bullets are blank.

In September of 1991, I was playing the role of a fellow named Bill Stiles, one of the gang members. My job was to ride in on my horse, shoot 'em up, get shot and die, and if all had gone well, this would not have been too difficult.

We always try to make everything look dramatic and authentic, but this time things got a little out of hand.

The first three guys rode into town, got off their horses, walked around town, and went in the bank. The second two came in. One got off his horse and stood in front of the bank to guard it, and the other one stood out in the street. Then the third wave came in and just rode up and down the street.

Historically speaking, two raiders died on the street. My job was to make sure there was only one raider on the ground, and if that was the case, I was supposed to die. In these tumultuous seven-minute live performances, anything can happen, including somebody falling off his horse. So if there were two gangsters on the ground, I was supposed to let them die, and I was just supposed to stay on my horse and leave.

Only one guy was down, so it was my turn to die. The re-enactment was almost over so I fell off my horse. I was supposed to stay whichever way I landed when I fell--whether on my back or on my stomach--because the character is supposed to be dead when he lands on the ground.

I happened to fall on my stomach, and I was carrying two six-shooters. The one on my right was in my hand, and I'd used up all my shots. At that time we were using brass casings and just loading them down with black powder so we'd get a nice flame, loud noise, and plenty of smoke.

When the raid is over, traditionally the townspeople or spectators come over to the fallen raiders, turn them over, and claim victory. To this day, we don't know what went wrong, but when they started to roll me over, my left holstered six-shooter .357 went off.

The one chamber that went off was all fire in the holster, so it ignited the other five. They all went off--with all their flame. Because of those five, the fire went up to my gun belt, where I had another eleven rounds. These eleven all caught fire and blew up around my waist.

My wife said that the rapid series of explosions raised me about three inches off the ground. Someone rolled me on my back, and the crowd started pointing and laughing as the smoke spread everywhere. In shock, I jumped up and started putting fires out. At this point, audience members realized that the fire was not part of the act and that I was in serious danger.

I tried to put out the fire on the duster I wore, but it flared up again. Utimately I had to throw it on the ground and stomp up and down on it. Then I folded it up, put it on the back of the saddle, got back onto my horse, and rode off.

I went to the hospital, where they treated me for severe burns and bruises. Thanks to the effectiveness of modern drugs, and my belief that the show must go on, I was able to announce the drum and bugle corps competition that night.

But when I rode in the parade as my character the following year, I devised a little sight gag. For the benefit of those who had either seen or heard about my incident the year before, I carried a fire extinguisher hidden under my duster. As I rode along, I lifted the duster and showed my historically inaccurate outlaw gear. Those who got the joke roared with laughter, and those who hadn't heard my story were very perplexed.

Wayne Eddy is a radio announcer on KYMN in Northfield and Chairman of the Board of the Pavek Museum of Broadcasting in St. Louis Park.

When I Was 4 on the Farm in Walnut Grove
by Lavonne Johnson Swanson

We moved to the big farm
where my Grandma and Grandpa had lived
with the big Belgian workhorses named Topsy and Ike
and with the big red barn filled with hay and cows
and kittens that drank warm milk
from a pan my father filled with four squirts
from the cow's teats
and if any of us kids were around,
he'd give us a squirt too.

We didn't have just cows though
we had chickens and ducks and pigs
not little pigs but big mean pigs
that made my Grandpa so mad
he'd chase them around the pen yelling "hatfadumadajit!"
He didn't think I knew
that was a Belgian swear word for "sonofabitch."

My big sisters did all the work
like picking lady bugs off potato plants
and putting them in kerosene cans
and carrying the slop pail from under the sink
out to the pig trough,
and they had to take care of me,
and sometimes we'd sweep the ground
around the trees in the grove
and they'd help me make mudpies.

At supper my sister Kathryn
would make me sit at the table
until I cleaned my plate
no matter how much I cried and said I'd throw it up.
And then I would throw it up
and then she'd really be mad.
My sister Ihla brushed my hair and put ribbons in it.

My sister Betty was a cowgirl.
She had her own horse who was fast as lightning
and that's why she named him Lightning.
She was just plain crazy about that horse.
She'd brush him and feed him and talk to him
just like he was a real person.

One day she got it in her head
that she was going to do this trick
that she saw Gene Autry and Champion do.
She told me to go stand by the post
at the end of the driveway and just wait,
and then she got on her horse and gave him the spurs
and down the driveway they came galloping
and Betty swooped down and scooped me up so fast
and she held me under her arms-- my legs danglin' down
and we whirled around and dashed back up the driveway
and circled around the yard to the front porch
where my Mother was waiting
to give my sister a good scolding.

"Don't you know you could have killed your little sister?"
and "Do you want me to take that horse away from you?"
And she sent Betty to her room
and after awhile I climbed up the stairs to see her
and she was smilin' and feelin' proud
cause she could do the trick
just like in the movies.

Vonnie Johnson left Walnut Grove when she was 6 and lived in several southwestern Minnesota towns before moving to Albert Lea. She studied at Gustavus Adolphus and George Washington University and Minnesota State University. She enjoys gardening, rug braiding and the arts.

About Minnesota Memories

I lived in Minnesota for the first forty years of my life, and I will always consider myself a Minnesotan. After moving away, I always enjoyed getting together with fellow Minnesotans to share stories about life in the North Star State. These stories not only entertained, but they refreshed and restored whatever it was about me that needed restoration.

In 1998, I started teaching high school in Maryland, and across the hall I discovered another transplanted Minnesotan, Kathy Megyeri. When things got tense--as they often do when one is teaching high school English these days--I'd walk across the hall, and we would unwind by telling stories about people we grew up with and adventures we had before we moved away from a place we still feel connected to. Sometimes these conversations triggered such hilarity that people passing by wondered if we had flipped out.

One day, after Kathy had sold a story to the *Chicken Soup* publishers, I said, "Somebody should compile a book of stories about life in Minnesota. Every Minnesotan has at least one good true story or recollection, and if we compile all those stories, we could publish a terrific book." We pitched that idea to publishers, and they pitched it right back.

After recovering from this rejection, we decided that we would take it upon ourselves to compile a book of extraordinary stories by ordinary Minnesota folks. We contacted old classmates and friends, but only a few responded because many doubted that we would actually publish a book. Undaunted, we confounded those skeptics, wrote some of our own stories, combined them with a few we received from other people, and published *Minnesota Memories* in the summer of 2001.

I traveled more than 10,000 miles that summer, from Grand Marais to Austin and from Adrian to Winona--talking to newspaper reporters and radio interviewers about my *Minnesota Memories* mission. I spoke at county fairs, schools, class reunions, book stores, trade shows, and historical societies. I invited ordinary people to send their extraordinary stories for *Minnesota Memories 2*, and they responded by sending the stories in this book.

If you enjoyed reading *Minnesota Memories 2,* tell a friend and share the fun. This book and the original *Minnesota Memories* are available at most major book stores, many gift shops, by direct mail, on Amazon.com and at public libraries.

If you have a story you'd like to submit for the next volume, send it to the address printed below. I don't mind a few misspelled words or dangling participles. A good story is a good story, and if your story is good, I'll try to polish it up and put it in the next volume. An overwhelming response from storytellers all over Minnesota suggests that many more stories should be published in many more volumes. Here's your chance to become part of recorded history. I look forward to hearing from you.

Joan Claire Graham
Purveyor of Memories

Storytellers may submit true stories for *Minnesota Memories 3* to the address below. Inquiries about book talks and presentations at stores, organizations, historical societies, libraries, classes, reunions, get-togethers or events are also welcome.

To order *Minnesota Memories* or *Minnesota Memories 2*, send
$13.95 plus $3 postage & handling
Minnesota Memories
11505 Monongahela Drive
Rockville, Maryland 20852
Phone: 301-770-1259
Email: MinnMemory@aol.com
(no spaces between words or letters in email address)

Special Offer: *Minnesota Memories* & *Minnesota Memories 2*
$25 for both, postage included--Save $9!
Cash, checks to Minnesota Memories, or money orders accepted

About the Author

Joan Claire Graham graduated from Albert Lea High School, where she was profoundly influenced by journalism teacher Edna Gercken and theatre director Wally Kennedy.   After graduating from Winona State University in 1967, Joan taught high school English, speech, drama, and journalism. She wrote and directed plays and directed a cooperative pre-school. In addition to writing freelance articles, she has written family histories. Last year she co-authored and published *Minnesota Memories.* The mother of two incredibly talented, beautiful, and intelligent adult daughters, Joan lives in Maryland.